PRAISE FOR EMJAY SMITH

Ultimately, the book seems to suggest that we have a lot more power and authority over our destiny than many of us take advantage of. We should study to be more observant of systems, seasons, cycles and processes.

— ALPHONSO IVY, LICENSE PROFESSIONAL COUNSELOR & ASST. PASTOR-GROW 2 GROW CHRISTIAN CENTER

This book is very informative and well written. It's awesome how Mr. Smith uses Biblical principles to support his writings. It's very understandable on all levels. A great read!

— LATECIA CLAY, ENTREPRENEUR, INVESTOR

This is well done!

— OKCHI NAKNI ACHUKMA: EIL., TRIBAL CHIEF MINISTER

I love the way this book details how & why you should be living your best life. The author provides great tips you can use as a check list to achieve your individual goals.

— MELVIN DAVIS, BOYS & GIRLS CLUB DIRECTOR

I believe this will be an excellent primer for believers and unbelievers in terms of acquiring not just a working knowledge of SCSP, but the actual tools necessary to be a force in the Kingdom of God.... job well done!

— LATOUR WINSTON, HEALTHCARE SALES REP./ELDER/MINISTER

One thing that I keep reflecting on weekly (often daily) is the idea of planting seeds and how they root and multiply more seeds. This truth and practical use of this idea is not a new idea to me but the revelation comes with how I've applied you message to limiting the type of negative seeds that I allow to be placed in my mind, body, and spirit because just allowing the negative idea or person to root or manifest in you will allow negative to grow in you.

— KEITH TURNER, AUTHOR/ENTREPRENEUR/MOTIVATIONAL SPEAKER

This book is such a GREAT READ. My God, Marcus!

— RHONDA MCALISTER, AUTHOR/ENTREPRENEUR/SPEAKER

SYSTEMS, CYCLES, SEASONS, & PROCESSES

Understanding and Applying the Law of Seedtime and Harvest

EMJAY SMITH

Copyright © 2018 by Marcus "Emjay" Smith
Published by EduMatch®
PO Box 150324, Alexandria, VA 22315
www.edumatchpublishing.com

All rights reserved. No portion of this book may be reproduced in any form without permission from the publisher, except as permitted by U.S. copyright law. For permissions contact sarah@edumatch.org.

These books are available at special discounts when purchased in quantities of 10 or more for use as premiums, promotions fundraising, and educational use. For inquiries and details, contact the publisher: sarah@edumatch.org.

ISBN:

I'd like to dedicate this work, my first book to the memory of those special precious loved ones who are not present who I wish I could have shared this special accomplishment with.

To my beautiful mother of unconditional love: Arnita I. Silas. Thank you mama for making me. Your son has done what you always knew and believed I could accomplish. Words alone cannot express my love for you. I know you would be proud.

To my grandparents, Willie E. and Queen Esther Silas, Cleveland and Ethel Smith, Author Jones: thank you for being my foundation and being my examples for marriage.

To my aunts Andrea "Auntie Mae" Burns, Archie "Aunt Archie" Ingram, and my uncle Cleveland "Uncle Junior" Smith. Thank you for all you did for me while you were here for me and my cousins.

To my beautiful baby sister Monique "Lisa Marie" Smith. Babygirl, you were gone too soon but the boys are in good hands and will be well taken care of. Love you so much.

CONTENTS

Introduction	ix
Why I Wrote This Book	xvii
1. Seedtime And Harvest—The Law (The System Principle)	1
2. Obedience as a Seed	21
3. Time as a Seed	35
4. Faith as a Seed	47
5. Thoughts as a Seed	57
6. Words as a Seed	73
7. Sowing versus Giving Principle	81
8. Day and Night (The Cycle Principle)	95
9. Summer and Winter (The Season Principle)	107
10. The Journey (The Process Principle)	121
S.C.S.P. Summary	133
About the Author	141
Acknowledgments	143
References	145
Other EduMatch Titles	149

INTRODUCTION

In 2007, I heard God speak to me in my heart to write a book after reading Genesis 8:22. It reads: *While the earth remaineth, seedtime and harvest, cold and heat, summer, and winter, and day and night shall not cease (Genesis 8:22 King James Version).* The words "Systems, Cycles, Seasons, and Processes" (SCSP) seemed to leap off the page as I read this verse of scripture. I heard the words, "Systems, Cycles, Seasons, and Processes," but I saw the words *"Seedtime and harvest, cold and heat, summer and winter, and day and night shall not cease."* I was reading one thing on the pages with my eyes, but I heard something different in my heart. I listened to a set of principles and laws behind the words. At first, I didn't realize that I didn't have a clear understanding of what I was reading. I did, however, recognize that there was some connection between what I saw with my eyes and what I heard in my heart.

Repetitious exposure, reading, and familiarity with the scriptures has a way of convincing you that you already know or understand everything that you read from the scriptures. I thought I did. Before this encounter, I had been the Production Director for a

Christian radio station for six years and produced Bible teaching programs for eight hours per day, five days per week. Although my job was to produce local, national, and international programs in fifteen, thirty, and sixty-minute segments, I was secretly using that time as my supplemental bible study time. I enjoyed learning the word, learning the principles taught, reading the stories of the heroes of faith, and learning how to apply the truths from the bible to my life. During this time, my wife and I would watch and listen to Bible teaching programs at night on various television networks seven days a week. We were members of one of the fastest-growing Bible-believing churches in the Midwest, which focused on teaching the word of God line upon line and precept upon precept, and we had been active members of our church since the year 2000. We attended church services multiple days of the week, served in various areas of the ministry, and listened to our pastor teach the word of God like no one we had ever heard in our city. Therefore, hearing him teach at various times and using Genesis 8:22 was nothing new for me. A hundred times or more, I would listen to the pastor quote this verse of scripture. So, I thought I knew and understood Genesis 8:22.

But for some reason, in 2007, the scripture seemed different to me. The scripture seemed to be speaking to me as if God wanted me to see or learn something new that my pastor had not already taught me, or something that I had never noticed. I wrote down in my prayer journal four words, which I believed God was giving to me as the title for a book I was to begin writing. The title would be *Systems, Cycles, Seasons, and Processes*. I was excited and terrified at the same time because I recognized there was something significant about these words, and the fact that he was bringing them to my attention meant that I needed to understand the definition of these words. I believed that there might be a revelation from the word of God regarding these four words. I also knew, however, that I did not want to approach the idea of writing a book based on any principle from the word of God, lightly or carelessly. I figured, if I'm going to do this, I better do it right, and I had better get started writing the book. There were just a few problems. First, I had no clue where to begin writing. Second, I had never written a book before. Third, no one knew who I was, and I didn't believe I had the credentials necessary to write a book on biblical principles that would be taken seriously. Lastly, I wasn't sure if I was the person that should be writing a book. After several weeks of overcoming the internal conflict in my mind, I started writing, but everything I was writing was terrible. I made several attempts to write a book on a subject that I thought I had little personal knowledge about, to help God knows who, with no expertise of my own. What I was writing had no substance, no insight, no revelation, no learning, no edifying, or anything of value to others. I wrote pages of nothingness that sounded like an intellectual was having a conniption. What I wrote down didn't speak to me, and I knew that it would not connect with others. So finally, after a few more attempts, I put the book writing down; for ten years. I decided not to write anything until I at least had a clear idea of what to write and how to write it. All I had was four words.

During that time, I looked for teachings from other ministers, pastors, and teachers in the body of Christ who could give me clues or some foundational principles I could glean from to know what I was supposed to be writing or where to begin. I began researching the words systems, cycles, seasons, and processes. I would investigate anything and everything I could find on these topics to give me a starting point. By now, you would think that if God was telling me to write a book, that I should talk to him to get some direction and clarity. Initially, I didn't. In my mind, if he told me to do it, then I thought I was the one that needed to do the work. As you can probably imagine, I didn't get too far with anything of any merit. Eventually, I attempted to pray to get some clarity, but I really didn't seek God's heart in the book.

A few years went by, and I picked up the task again in 2017 and started writing what I believed was a much better version of the book to address this concept of Systems, Cycles, Seasons, and Processes. By this time, I seemed to have had a few pages of some decent content that people might have an interest in, and that might reveal the truths God wanted me to share. At this point, I had done a lot of meditation and research on systems, cycles, seasons, and processes. I discovered what these words meant from an ecological, engineering, technological, and economic perspective, but I had not moved the needle on writing the book. I did not write for about a year. It was then that my wife started reading through my prayer journal and found instructions from God on many things I am supposed to accomplish in my lifetime. Among some of the instructions she found were instructions to write this book, but the emphasis in my prayer journal was different than what I had been writing. My beautiful wife discovered that the focus of the book I was writing was different than the instructions received. I was writing about systems, cycles, seasons, and processes and how things work in business, economics, and finance.

I believed I was on the right track because, in 2005, the Lord instructed me to study two subjects: *The Kingdom of God* and the *world's financial system*. I was noticing how many people, especially God's people, were struggling financially and unnecessarily because there was little to no education on money in the church, except on tithing and giving. Notice that I said that there was little to no education on the subject, except tithing and giving. I saw how many people were struggling to make ends meet and how churches tended to shy away from the discussion about money unless it specifically dealt with tithing and giving. There weren't many sermons on saving, investing, budgeting, cash flow management retirement, entrepreneurship, asset protection, wealth accumulation, or anything else revolving around fiscal management. That's not to say that no one else was doing it, but from my own experience of working in Christian radio, and my interactions with thousands of ministers, pastors, and Bible teachers in my city, as well as not hearing these things on Christian television or radio programs, it seemed that no one was talking about it. They appeared to be uncomfortable or unwilling to have a practical discussion about the subject of money. They would regularly solicit funds from those that listened to their programs to support them financially and quoted scriptures about how God would bless them financially for doing so. Maybe they were ignorant about sound financial principles and lacked understanding about the subject even though they ardently preached that others should give. Perhaps that's why they were reluctant to teach it. Occasionally you might hear someone mention stewardship, but that's about all they might do, mention it. It also appeared that most discussions about money in the church would turn negative, and those raising valid points about it or the lack of it among God's people were deemed to be heretics. You might have other pastors who would discuss how much God had blessed them materially and financially but didn't provide their members with practical teaching on how to duplicate the same lifestyle or standard of living in the lives of their members. For example, those ministers, pastors, and Bible teachers who taught ideas like God wants his people to prosper materially and financially were labeled "prosperity" preachers. This type of preaching appealed to many who lacked financial stability but enraged others who didn't agree with this theological view. Then you might have a few "ministers" who would use the scriptures to manipulate their congregations so that they might live lavishly off the freewill offerings of their devoted members. Maybe they were afraid of being sued for "stealing" or misappropriating church funds. Whatever the reason was, there seemed to be a love-hate relationship with the subject of money; preachers loved to ask for it, and members hated to hear about it. From my research, I began to see the relationship between business, economics, and financial systems, and that became my focus.

During this period, I had started teaching financial literacy to at-risk youth as part of an afterschool program for about eight years. At the time, I believed that financial literacy, along with entrepreneurship and economic empowerment, would make a difference in distressed and blighted communities as well as among God's people. Based on my study of money, finance, economics, and the financial system, I began identifying biases that existed within this system and saw how people were negatively affected by it. I had read numerous books, watched countless documentaries, and attended seminars on these subjects. I learned about the factors that drove, influenced, and shaped the economy as well as learned about the different phases and shifts that transformed it like agriculture, industrialization, information, technology, and innovation. I learned about various methods to make money, the relationship between debt and wealth creation, and why the rich get richer, and the poor stay poor no matter what they do. I read several books on the formation of the Federal Reserve, central banking, and the process of fractional reserve lending, and how it was systematically dispossessing people of their wealth, property, and legal rights. I studied the Constitution and other founding documents of this nation regarding the relationship between property ownership and the protection of their rights in courts of law. I read books regarding asset protection, tax avoidance, as well as cash flow and wealth management and began to see the connection between law and commerce. I also learned how wealthy people were able to hide behind corporations, generate massive profits, pay little to nothing in taxes, and control the flow of resources they had without legally owning them, minimizing their liability to lawsuits and passing wealth down from generation to generation. These things helped me to realize that without this kind of knowledge, people would be systematically and permanently locked into their socio-economic status and be dependent on the government for life, even with advanced college degrees. I began to recognize that these subjects were not taught in most schools, and most people, like myself, were woefully ignorant of these subjects. At times I would listen to discussions, disagreements, and arguments at family events on politics and socio-economic issues. I would listen to liberal and conservative radio stations and television talk-show hosts discussing economics and public policy. I would also listen to a lively conversation among elected officials and other political pundits discuss social issues and never bring up how people were truly being impacted since economics decided the outcomes.

As I was learning about the economic system and getting my education on financial matters, the financial crisis of 2008 hit and caught many people off guard. We all saw how people had lost their jobs, hard-earned pensions, their homes, and in the cases of some small business owners, their businesses. We simultaneously watched CEO's receive bonuses called "golden parachutes" as compensation, while shareholders of the same companies received huge dividend payouts as their companies filed for Chapter 11 bankruptcy protection. We also saw an increase of new millionaires, multimillionaires, and new billionaires emerge from this crisis while Congress demanded taxpayers to underwrite a $700 billion bailout for companies on the verge of collapse and created new legislation to prevent the need for further bailouts. I realized that all this was not just the by-product of greed, but also the by-product of systems. I realized the crisis was a transference of wealth through the stock exchange from the hands of everyday people into the hands of the wealthy who hid behind multinational corporations and conglomerates.

I also discovered that the 2008 crisis was only one of several recurring events that happened before in cycles in U.S. history, as well as in other nations where there had been a central banking system. These systems were controlling the lives and decisions of people across the country, occurred in predictable cycles every few years while going through the various seasons and processes necessary to repeat again. Lastly, I recognized for people to get ahead financially, they needed to know or acknowledge the seasons to invest and grow their money, whether in a bull or bear market.

Aha! I finally found the secret to why people across the country were struggling to make ends meet. I was beginning to understand why the middle class was shrinking and joining the ranks of those now classified as low income or those living at or below the poverty line. We witnessed this same group of Americans bearing the bulk of the tax burden and scrambling to hold on to some sense of security and their sanity. I found out that the world financial system was fixed, and the banks, the government, and big corporations were pulling the financial strings of the GDP (gross domestic product) of nations.

Now armed with this new insight, I thought I found the answer God wanted me to know and was ready to share it with others. After all, financial literacy, financial education, and economic empowerment were the answer, right? I believed that the only thing people needed was the correct information about how the financial system worked, right? Wrong! Yes, people were being affected by an intricately designed system that has been in existence for several hundreds of years, dating back to the era of kings and kingdoms; but money was not and is not their main problem. If money or the lack of it is not their main problem, then what is the problem? The problem for me, as far as writing the book was concerned, was that my focus was still wrong. God wanted me to see that the problem was not economic alone, but rather a lack of proper stewardship over one's resources, and TRUST IN THE WRONG SYSTEM. The Lord began to reveal to me that the answer people needed and the focus for the book, centered around the scriptures and God's way of doing things. The answer is found in Genesis 8:22, which is also the foundation of the book.

WHY I WROTE THIS BOOK

Systems, Cycles, Seasons, and Processes is written because, first and foremost, God told me to do it. Second, it is written to help people like me, who have struggled in any area of their lives trying to find happiness, fulfillment in life, or discover their purpose in life. Third, it is written to help people identify the principles and laws that they have turned on or activated in their own lives that might be working against them, causing them to experience frustration, loss, and suffering. Lastly, it is written to provide a blueprint on how certain principles and laws in God's kingdom work so that you will know what they are and how to apply them in your daily life to experience God-ordained success without dependence upon the world system. As we go on this journey, you will see lots of scriptures and stories that will illustrate and address specific points, principles, and precepts necessary for you to grasp what S.C.S.P. is all about. These principles are vital for you to identify, capture, document, list, and begin to put them into practice in your own life. The principles may seem to be easy and simple, and they are. However, because they are simple and easy, they are also easy to miss, dismiss, ignore, and reject. It is for that reason that I will be emphasizing them to you, the reader, throughout this book, so that you don't miss them.

Over the years in my search for truth, I have discovered that some of the most potent and profound concepts and principles in life go unnoticed because they are simple and easy to miss. As you read and learn, make sure you implement what you learn from this book. The book of Proverbs 4:7 states: Wisdom is the principal thing; therefore, get wisdom, and with all thy getting get understanding. Luke chapter 7:35 states, *"wisdom is justified of all her children."* In other words, wisdom is validated by its results. As you become aware of the principles shared in this book, take notes and prepare to start implementing them. Make the necessary corrections and adjustments. Then, apply the principles and prepare to experience the results in your own life.

1

SEEDTIME AND HARVEST—THE LAW (THE SYSTEM PRINCIPLE)

One of the first things the scriptures address in Genesis 8:22 is the atmosphere where this principle of seedtime and harvest operates. It states: *"While the earth remains."* This short statement means the principle of seedtime and harvest operates on earth and will always work, as long as the earth remains. It also says this principle will work anywhere on planet earth. What is the principle? The FIRST principle is that **Seedtime and harvest....shall not cease**. That's it! Seedtime and harvest shall not cease or will not stop and always works without fail. What is seedtime and harvest? Seedtime and harvest is the law and principle created by God to produce whatever you may need or want on earth by planting a seed, nurturing that seed, exercising patience during the growth process of that seed, and reaping the harvest of the crop. This principle is so simple that it is easy to ignore or dismiss as unnecessary information. Many people think of this principle as being something that only farmers or gardeners need to know. This principle says seedtime and harvest shall not cease. There are only two ways it will not work; first, if the earth no longer remains, and second, if the seed is not being sown. That means from generation to generation, from age to age, this principle will always exist, and it will still work for anyone on planet earth. We can say it another way. Seedtime and harvest **IS A LAW**. That means it will work anywhere, anytime, for anyone. Spiritual laws and laws of nature are not impartial. A law is always at work and will affect anyone and everyone that cooperates with it or violates it.

Maybe you will have a greater appreciation for this principle once you realize the significance of what I call the **Law of the Seed**. This law is stated in Genesis 1:11-12. It states: *And God said, Let the earth bring forth grass, the herb yielding seed, and the fruit tree yielding fruit after his kind, whose seed is in itself, upon the earth; and it was so. And the earth brought forth grass, and herb yielding seed after his kind, and the tree yielding fruit, whose seed was in itself, after his kind and God saw it was good.* These scriptures explain and highlight two points: the first point is that **EVERY SEED BRINGS FORTH FRUIT AFTER ITS OWN KIND**. The second point is that the **SEED IS IN ITSELF**. These scriptures reveal the LAW OF THE SEED, a powerful principle on earth. The law of the seed means a seed, any seed, will produce a harvest after its own kind, and the harvest also contains the potential of producing more seed within itself. This means **IT IS SELF-PERPETUATING** and will not stop producing unless someone stops planting the seed. This law will work for anyone with any kind of seed. This means a seed will produce a harvest, which produces fruit that contains seeds, which will become a greater harvest that produces more fruit with more seeds, and the process continues to repeat.

Something else to consider is that the harvest of any seed sown will always be greater than the seed that is planted. For example, one seed of corn can produce a stalk of corn with many ears of corn on the stalk. If you plant multiple seeds of corn into a field, it will produce a field of multiple stalks of corn with many ears of corn. The same is true for watermelons, mangos, or other fruits and vegetables that contain much seed. When those seeds are planted, they always produce a much larger harvest than the original seed(s) planted. Seedtime and harvest will always work because seeds are designed by God to be perpetual, producing agents of a particular kind of harvest. Another factor to consider here is the importance of the environment where seeds are planted. A seed must be planted in fertile soil to produce a bountiful harvest. The soil must be conducive to producing life if the soil is to be considered good soil. If the soil is no good, the seed might not germinate and produce a harvest. In other words, the soil must allow the seed to release its potential into the soil to produce abundance. Something else to consider is you must be able to recognize the seed(s) you have and the best place to plant your seed(s). If you are unaware of the seeds you possess, you run the risk of not taking advantage of planting your seed when it needs to be planted and where it should be planted. These points are not being shared to encourage you to become a farmer, but they are being shared to help you recognize how these laws and principles work first so that you will know them, recognize them when they are at work, and be able to apply the principles in other areas of your life. Allow me to stress a few things here to you so that you don't miss them. First, **ALL SEEDS NEED SOIL TO PRODUCE A HARVEST, and NO SOIL CAN PRODUCE A HARVEST WITHOUT SEEDS.**

IN THE CASE of the human species, the seed (sperm) of a man needs the soil (womb) of a woman to produce a harvest called a baby, and the soil (womb) of a woman cannot produce a baby without the seed (sperm) of a man. As elementary as this may be, it must be stated that man's seed does not work with or mix with the soil of a field. The womb of a woman is not conducive to the seed of an animal or anything else that is not of the human species. Animals that are not of the same species cannot produce offspring with those of a different species. Seeds necessary for growing crops will not produce a harvest in the womb of a woman or any other mammal, yet every seed and species produce after their own kind. Spoken words do not produce a harvest in a field of freshly plowed soil, yet the seed of your words and all other seeds produce after their own kind when planted in the right soil. Word seeds must be sewn into the hearts of men, women, and children to produce a harvest. The word (seed) of a man that releases and produces confidence, boldness, and greatness, or timidity, hatred, and loyalty in the lives of people must all have their place in the hearts of men to have any effect. The effect of those words in a persons' life is dependent upon the potential of the seed carrying the words and the receptivity of the soil (the person's heart) to the seed. This principle is critical to consider regarding planting seed and the importance of protecting your heart (soil) from the wrong kinds of seeds. Your seed could be money or capital for an investment in some sort of investment product or a startup company. Your seed could be nurturing, cultivating, or mentoring young people, or grooming the successor of your company or empire. Proverbs 4:23 states: keep (guard/protect) your heart with all diligence; for out of it are the issues of life.

This is necessary to understand because, through your thoughts, words, and actions, you can allow certain seeds (words) to enter your heart (mind), and those seeds (thoughts) can begin to germinate and produce an unwanted harvest in your life. For example, Matthew 12:35 states: A good man out of the good treasure of his heart brings forth good things, and an evil man out of the evil treasure of his heart brings forth evil things. This verse is explaining that the heart of a man is just like the soil of a farm that can produce an intentional harvest and has the potential to repeat production. This means your heart (mind) can produce a harvest in your life, for something wanted, or even something unwanted. The key factor here is that your heart (mind) is the soil that will produce a harvest of things based on the seed you plant or allow to be planted into it. If you choose to plant good seed, a good harvest will result, but the opposite is also true, and if you aren't careful, you might end up with a harvest that you did not intend simply because your heart was receptive to it. This also means that you can plant a seed into your own heart (mind) intentionally through reading, listening, or speaking and begin to produce a harvest in your life from what you planted. This is exactly what people do who are in the personal development business do. They intentionally plant positive thinking seeds into their hearts and saturate themselves with the possibility, thinking about that content daily. This drives out negative or unwanted thoughts, and they begin thinking, speaking, and producing positive results simply because they think it is possible. You can use this principle in the same manner as a farmer who plants his seed into his field to produce a harvest. In other words, you could grow, in your own life, a harvest from the seeds you plant into your own heart the same way a farmer plants corn and harvests stalks of corn. It is intentional and on purpose.

Now the seeds I am referring to are thoughts, ideas, or suggestions. You must know and understand this because the enemy of your soul understands this and can use your own heart (mind) to grow unwanted thoughts, ideas, and suggestions, which in turn becomes a harvest of unwanted activities, events, and consequences produced in your life. The enemy may use your parents, siblings, teachers, coaches, bosses, elected officials, or others in authority of you to plant certain kinds of seeds in your heart or the heart of the masses through mediums such as radio, television, print media, film, or streaming services via the internet. If you don't think or believe this is true, then examine your own life. Are you thinking, speaking, and experiencing negative because you think, speak, and do positive things, or is it the opposite? If you are experiencing negative in your life, check what you are reading, listening to, or who and what you are exposing yourself to regularly. It is inconsistent with saturating your ears, heart, and mind with negativity and negative not be produced in your life, and the opposite is also true as well. If you watch or listen to local news, more than half of it is negative and depressing because it mostly reports a crime, murder, and negativity. The principle here is that faith comes by hearing. If you hear negative most of the time, you might have a negative outlook on life. These seeds are constantly producing a harvest year after year in the lives of people, and because their minds have been cultivated to think a certain way and produce the same old results, they keep getting the same results. Therefore, it becomes necessary to change the seeds being planted. Let me add this, because the process is gradual and subtle, it seems harmless, but habits are gradual and subtle, and before you know it, you are thinking, speaking, or doing something that you have no idea why you are doing it, how it started, or where it came from, but it is all the by-product of seedtime and harvest.

One other thing to consider is that a seed operates as <u>A SYSTEM</u>. This was the first revelation from the title Systems, Cycles, Seasons, and Processes I saw when reading Genesis 8:22. The Lord gave me an understanding of what a system is. He said to me, "<u>A system is a specific method of operation that creates order, produces efficiency, creates leverage, is controllable, duplicatable, can be used to create wealth, operates automatically, can be used to manage resources, creates time freedom, and provides options.</u>" You might be thinking, how can a seed be a system? First of all, the seed creates the order within the soil once it is planted. This is by design. Second, the seed undergoes an efficient process to produce a harvest; this is by design. Third, the seed absorbs the resources of the soil and utilizes it for its benefit, demonstrating leverage; this is by design. Fourth, the seed releases its potential into the soil and dominates the spot where the seed was planted, giving it control of the environment until the harvest; this is by design. Next, the seed produces after its kind, which is duplication by design. Then the seeds themselves can create wealth by monetizing the seeds or by selling the harvest. Either way can produce wealth, which is by design. When the seed is planted, it develops a root system and stem with little assistance from the one planting the seed. This is by design. Next, the seed manages the resources of moisture, minerals in the soil, and sunlight to grow and mature. As the seed goes through this germination process, the farmer or planter can use his or her time to do other things, allowing for time freedom and other options for the planter. All of this is by design.

One characteristic I would like to highlight here about systems is their ability to be duplicatable or to be replicated. Systems are important to understand because systems are designed to produce specific, intentional results that can be duplicated. Systems are designed to be replicable so that whatever the system produces can be duplicated anywhere and anytime. Just as a seed will produce after its kind, a system is designed to replicate results. Think of it this way: **ALL SYSTEMS PRODUCE THE RESULTS THEY ARE DESIGNED TO PRODUCE**. Even if the outcome is not intended, the system will still produce what it was designed to produce. This is important to know because if you intend to produce a specific result, it is necessary to know how to produce that result; otherwise, you will get something other than what you intended. At the sake of sounding redundant, I will state it this way: when you are designing a system, be sure of what outcome you want to produce because you might get something you do not want. Look at the financial system, what kind of results does it produce? Look at the educational system, what kind of results does it produce? Look at the healthcare system, what kind of results does it produce? Whether the results are intentional or not, the system will always produce what it was designed to produce. In this way, seeds and systems are alike. Also, consider that seedtime and harvest is not only a law, but it is also a system, God's system for dominion in the earth.

Here is another principle the Lord shared with me: Systems are the key to dominion in the earth. Think about this statement: Systems are the KEY to DOMINION in the earth. Don't miss this point. Systems are God's idea. Systems create order, and this is why the scripture says: Let all things be done, decent and in order. When you think of a system, think of a structure. Something that is built to last is a structure, and what helps to sustain the structure is the infrastructure. That infrastructure creates order, and order is the by-product of a system. In other words, everything you want to do needs to be done using a system if you expect to have good success and if you want to keep it decent and in order. The scriptures also state that God is not the author of confusion, which means whenever there is confusion, there is no order, and where there is a lack of order, there is no system in place.

The most successful businesses in the world have figured this out. They all use systems to dominate the marketplace with their goods, products, or services. Even if they are not the biggest company, they will use systems to corner the market in their niche. Whenever you see anyone in the earth who is ruling and reigning like a king in this life, you are watching someone who has learned to design, build, master, and utilize systems. Systems guarantee success; that is, systems always produce the results they are designed to produce repeatedly. The reason for this is systems create order, produce efficiency, provide leverage, give you control, allow you to duplicate results, they operate automatically, they manage resources, create wealth, and give you time freedom, which gives you options to do other things. If you have a business, you have a system. If you have an organization, you have a system. If you have an institution, you have a system. If you have a church, you have a system. If you run a government, you have a system. If you are the head of a nation or a country, you have a system. On planet earth, the world has multiple systems that integrate one with another, and they all must abide by the same general set of rules and standards. Those rules and standards are part of the world system.

Another point to consider is that systems are neutral but are molded and shaped by the designer of the system or by the person in charge. In other words, systems can be amoral, but depending on what industry (system) it is may determine what goal, what harvest, or what endgame will result. But regardless of the industry, remember this point: SYSTEMS ARE THE KEY TO DOMINION IN THE EARTH. God's Kingdom is a system, and those who choose to operate in his system will experience the results that his system is designed to produce. When you learn about God's Kingdom (System) and how to apply his principles, it becomes hard to go back to living life how you used to. You begin to realize that regardless of what happens in any part of the world, God's Kingdom (System) is superior to all others and will always produce greater results than what the world's system can produce, with no sorrow added to it. This does not mean the world system doesn't produce tangible results, but it means that sorrow and stress come along with those results when you implement the principles of the world system.

Systems have the potential to reproduce and duplicate for generations without end unless they are not used. You will know exactly what the outcome will be and how long it will take and what the harvest or outcome will be. Anyone can utilize this principle to achieve success with any kind of seed or system and get specific, intentional harvests or specific, intentional results. Why is this important you might ask? Consider these two simple but powerful points; <u>ALL SEEDS</u> AND <u>ALL SYSTEMS</u> operate by this same principle. <u>EVERY SEED PRODUCES AFTER ITS OWN KIND. EVERY SEED!</u> <u>EVERY SYSTEM PRODUCES WHAT THEY ARE</u>

DESIGNED TO PRODUCE. EVERY SYSTEM! Also, <u>EVERY SEED HAS SEED IN ITSELF</u>.

Seed can refer to fruit, vegetables, animals, humans, acts of kindness and charity, or acts of evil and crimes. Think of it this way, **every time a seed is sown, a law is set into motion: <u>the law of the seed</u>**. Also, **every time a system is turned on, something is being duplicated or replicated.** Sir Issac Newton's Third Law of Motion says it this way; "for every action, there is an equal and opposite reaction" ("Newton's Third Law," n.d.). Mr. Newton is describing the operation of a law that God created. The Bible calls it seedtime and harvest. A quote erroneously attributed to Albert Einstein said it this way: Insanity is doing the same thing over and over but expecting different results (Ruitt, 2018). Mr. Einstein is describing the operation of a system.

Newton is describing the operation of a law. The law is called seedtime and harvest, and what Einstein is describing is the operation of a system. Both are necessary for you to know. This principle can also apply to Proverbs 26:2, which states in part, *the curse causeless shall not come*. What this means is a curse (violation of a law=empowerment to fail) will not happen or occur without a cause or reason. The cause is a seed sown. The seed could be a decision to do a certain thing, act a certain way, or move in a certain direction. This is important to comprehend because when negative things occur, in many cases, it can be traced back to a seed sown: a seed of error, a seed of disobedience, a seed of rebellion, a seed of delay, a seed of dishonor, etc. A decision can lead in a direction to a predetermined destination that was unintended. That same decision was the seed that produced the harvest of loss, pain, or destruction in the life of the person.

APPLYING THE SYSTEM PRINCIPLE

I have an acquaintance of mine who always likes to think outside the box, but at the same time, is logical and practical about his decision making. We'll call him BJ. BJ likes to say, "but how do I make this work"? Or "how do I apply this"? In other words, whenever someone gives him information about something that has the potential to help him or others solve a problem, he would say, I want to know how do I apply this information? Don't give me all the details, just the basics. These are fundamental questions to pose to anyone claiming they have a business or investment opportunity, a new invention, some new gadget, or a solution to a problem affecting the masses. When it comes to applying the principle of systems to your own life, it is necessary to understand the purpose and design of the system to know how it works.

PRINCIPLE 1. Find a system that produces the kind of results you want to be duplicated in your own life, or create, design, and implement your own system.

HOW TO APPLY PRINCIPLE 1. To implement your own system, decide on the kinds of results you want to achieve for any area of your life, for example, losing weight. First, research what a healthy weight is for you and the principles of health necessary for you to implement for your body to be healthy. Next, you can research online by going to Google or YouTube or talk to a health or medical professional. This point is very important because many people do not know their numbers. Knowing your numbers refers to knowing your weight, blood pressure, heart rate, BMI (body mass index), glucose levels, pH balance levels (potential hydrogen), and other pertinent information. I know there will be a lot of information to go through, but something you should keep in mind is to look for information that is foundational to health and consistent across the board. Look for information related to nutrition, exercise, hydration, stress reduction, proper rest, proper sleep, etc. I have heard it stated many times by professionals in this arena to focus your attention on being healthy because a healthy body will lose weight. Your body is God's temple, so make sure you know how to care for it and understand what health is, what it looks like for you, and what your body requires to be healthy. Once you understand these foundational principles and understand what results you want to achieve, decide where you want to begin, how you want to proceed, and give yourself a deadline to achieve your desired results. Write down the objectives that will support the results you want and then work your way backward. Be patient with yourself, and be consistent. Please be flexible and adjust your plan when needed.

My acquaintance BJ would say you should start with the end in mind or start with the results you want and then work your way backward. It's referred to as reverse engineering. This is what God does; he begins with the end in mind and works his way backward. The bible says it this way, declaring the end from the beginning[10]. If you remember from our definition of a system, it is a method of operation that first creates order, produces efficiency, creates leverage, is controllable, can duplicate results, is used to create wealth, is automated, can manage resources, provides time freedom and gives you options to do other things. Any system that can create order or can restore order to an environment is something worth knowing and learning about because the ability to create or restore order to an environment is power. To create or restore order, your system must have the ability to eliminate chaos, confusion, and disorder because this is what systems do. Systems enable you to transform a desert into Las Vegas. Systems and imagination transformed thousands of acres of swampland into Disney World in Orlando, Florida.

Principle 2. Have a definite starting point and a definite ending point to produce the product, service, or results you want.

How to apply Principle 2. Decide when you want to begin and end your process by setting dates or creating a window of time for when you want to start applying the principle, and by what date you expect to see results. For example, if you start implementing health principles today, give yourself three to six months to the date you started so that you can observe and measure your results.

Principle 3. Your system must have the ability to produce results efficiently, making things easier, better, and faster; this is what systems do.

How to apply Principle 3. Your system should make things easier, run smoother, eliminating extra or unnecessary work or tasks, producing measurable results. This will help you stay motivated as you see and experience things moving in the desired direction, so once you create and implement your system, check to make sure your system is producing the results you want. You may need to adjust your system in some way, so be flexible and patient. For example, if you are implementing your system but realize your body is tired a lot, but you are eating right, you may be overdoing it and not getting the proper rest, enough water, or you may be stressed. Maybe the area that needs adjusting is the amount of sleep that you are not getting enough of. You may need to rework your daily schedule to make sure you are getting proper sleep every night. It could be any number of things, but the point here is to make sure you recognize how well your system is working for you and if the results you are getting are easier, better, and faster. Making things progress smoother, easier, better, and faster gives you efficiency.

Principle 4. Your system must have the ability to create leverage.

How to Apply Principle 4. If you want leverage, for example, in fitness training, you may want to incorporate superset weight training along with cardio. This method allows for muscle conditioning, body sculpting, fat burning, and building endurance all at once while also reducing workout time. Another suggestion would be to utilize mobile fitness equipment that goes where you go allowing you to workout anywhere and everywhere, and you control what you do and how long you work out. This allows your workout time to be reduced while receiving the benefits of a total body workout and maintaining consistency in your routine.

When you think about leverage, think of something small moving something much larger than itself and doing it with ease. The rudder of a ship is significantly smaller than the ship itself yet can change the direction of the ship. The captain uses the steering wheel of his ship, which is connected to the hydraulic system, to turn and control the direction of the multi-ton water vessel on the sea. Without the leverage that the rudder provides, control of the ship would be significantly limited. As your system begins to produce the leverage you want, you will begin to work smarter and not harder because your system will be maintaining the leverage you built. This is the power of leverage, and leverage is a function of systems.

PRINCIPLE 5. Your system must give you the ability to control the process and outcomes at will.

HOW TO APPLY PRINCIPLE 5. For example, for your wellness plan, your system/routine must allow you to lose six inches off your waistline through spinning thirty minutes a day, four days per week for two months, walking six miles a day, six-day per week for two months, and reducing body fat by twenty percent by eliminating processed foods, eliminating artificial sugar, and increasing water intake by thirty percent for two months. Your systems must allow you to control the process enabling you to obtain the results you want to achieve.

Systems allow you to determine what the outcome will be before you begin. Your system must have the ability to produce exactly what you want, as much as you want, as many times as you want, in a specific time frame, and serve as many people as you want. The manufacturing or assembling of an automobile is the function of systems, which is controllable. The McDonald's franchise business model and its BIG MAC are the results of systems which are also controllable. Structured education at all levels of learning is the result of systems that controls what people learn. Structured governments at the local, state, and federal levels are the result of systems that produce predictable results on purpose and are the result of controllable systems.

Once you have perfected the process of control with your system, you can now duplicate or replicate the results at will, and now you have the potential solution for serving the needs of others with your product, service, or system, which now becomes a business opportunity. This business opportunity enables you to add value to the lives of others while creating economic opportunities for yourself and for others, which now provides you with time freedom or options to do other things. Options or time freedom is the goal that many people allude to when describing what they call freedom. Somewhere in their definition or description of the ideal life is the concept of having one's time no longer under the control of another. This is especially true when a person has learned how to create the kinds of economic opportunities that no longer requires having a job or working for someone else. Having systems that can perform the tasks, duties, or daily operations of your work, business, or organization without your input while continuously generating unearned income is what most people want in life. For the many who can do this, refer to it as having a "laptop lifestyle." For others, this simply means no longer having to be in the "rat race" and now being able to think, breath, and live life on your terms, or at least being free enough and available to be and do what God wants you to.

This is one of the secrets that the rich, the wealthy, the powerful, and the well-connected use. They utilize systems in every area of their lives, enabling them to get more and more accomplished in life without having to do all of the work. This is the value of systems and why you must create, build, and use systems if you plan to rule and reign in life on the earth. So far, your system creates order, produces efficiency, creates leverage, controls a function or process, and can duplicate, or replicate results. The next element needed is the ability to be automated.

When something is automated, it can work on its own with no interference or assistance from anyone. As of the writing of this book, we are currently in the period of the greatest technological advancements in human history with technology disrupting every industry on the planet. It is referred to as the 4th *Industrial Revolution* or *Industry 4.0*. Because of this disruption, anything and everything that does manual work can now be replaced with artificial intelligence, "aka" robots, computers, and other technologies making the delivery of goods, products, and services automated or automatic requiring very little input from mankind to keep things moving. Examples of these innovations include the Tesla company, Mercedes-Benz, Ford Motor Company, GM, and other automotive manufacturers who are testing out autonomous vehicles on the roads and highways[11] (Mercer, Macaulay, Jun 27, 2019). These vehicles are known as self-driving cars, which no longer require a human being to operate the vehicle. These vehicles fitted with sophisticated hardware, software, smart-technology, and other sensors are enabling the age of *The Knight Rider* and *The Jetsons* to become a reality in our lifetime. These and other kinds of technologies are systems affecting our world. Many of these emerging technologies are also converging and becoming integrated, which creates a new set of variables to consider. For example, now these systems are utilizing many other resources that must be streamlined and managed effectively without becoming too expensive. Systems now are required to manage additional resources such as energy, fuel, data monitoring, collection, evaluation, sharing, troubleshooting, etc. So, with these innovations and advancements in technology, people and companies can replace or automate tasks, duties, and activities.

PRINCIPLE 6. Your system must have the capacity to be automated. In other words, it must be able to function with little to no effort from anyone.

HOW TO APPLY PRINCIPLE 6. Now that your health system is in place, you can incorporate technology to help automate your system. For example, no longer do you need to count calories, fat intake, fiber intake, etc. because there is software that can do that for you. The only effort required would be to check the data and taking the time to put data into the software. This can be done through a phone app or some other software. All you need to do is look at the data and make adjustments where needed.

Principle 7. Your system must have the ability to manage resources, allowing you the ability to free up time in other areas giving you your time back.

How to apply Principle 7. You must Identify the resources under your control and how you want to use them more efficiently. Prioritize which activities require your direct input, and delegate those that don't to others to complete. Invest in tools that help you free up your time. Seek out others to mentor you who successfully transitioned into freeing up their time and reduced their expenses and liabilities.

The entire process no longer requires your participation, and now you have options to do other, more meaningful things that your hearts or minds can contemplate. As these and other issues are resolved, managing resources will become a part of the process within the operating system. Once all of the components come together and are perfected, you will have established the foundation for a new level of evolution in your systems, which allows you to have your time back or having time freedom. Once the mechanisms are in place, you now can create wealth because you have something others need or desire, and you can provide it to them for a fee.

There is one final point about systems I would like to make. In the fourth chapters of Matthew and Luke, the Bible highlights a conversation between Jesus and Satan. In this account, the scripture tells us that Satan takes Jesus up on a high mountain and shows him all the kingdoms of the world in a moment. He then makes an offer to Jesus, saying he will give Jesus all the kingdoms of the world if he will simply bow down and worship him (Satan). Jesus rejects the offer and tells Satan that only God can be worshipped[14]. What is interesting in this exchange is that the Bible uses the word kingdoms to describe what Satan had control over, but when you think about what he was offering, you realize he (Satan) was talking about authority over systems. Satan was offering to give control of all the systems of the world to Jesus if he would worship him. When you look throughout the world today, everything is controlled by some kind of system because systems create order, produce efficiency, create leverage, are controllable, can duplicate results, are automated, can be used to manage resources, can be used to create wealth, and can provide time freedom allowing someone to have options in life.

2
OBEDIENCE AS A SEED

Throughout the Bible, the scriptures continually admonish the reader to hear and obey the written word of God as well as the voice of God. An act of obedience to the written word of God is intended to preserve, keep and protect your life from hurt, harm, and danger from the evil one (Prov. 3:5-6, Ps. 1:1-3). An act of obedience to the voice of God is intended to advance you into a new season of promotion and advancement in your life (Deut. 28:1-13, Job 36:11, Isa. 1:19). Every act of disobedience to the written word of God exposes you to sin, pain, attacks of the enemy, and loss (Deut. 28:16-69, Prov. 8:36, Job 36:12). Every act of disobedience to the voice of God causes you to experience delay and stagnation in your life, in your movement toward your purpose, your calling and your assignment in the Kingdom of God, and could negatively affect your destiny in Christ (1 Sam. 15:22-23). Both acts and actions of obedience and disobedience to the written word and the spoken word of God are seeds you sow to determine the harvest you reap (Gal. 6:7). Therefore, you must choose wisely what seeds you want to sow in your life (Jos. 24:15). Here is another principle to understand: sowing and reaping generally do not occur in the same season. Each natural season lasts three months, with a total of four seasons within one year. Sowing or planting occurs in the spring, and harvest occurs at the end of the summer leading into the fall. The exception to this rule is tropical environments. However, spiritually speaking, the law of seedtime and harvest can happen at any time and in the same season. The reason for this phenomenon is that when God instructs you to do a thing, he is inviting you to participate in his system of blessing, which is not limited by time, space, or matter. When you obey his instruction(s), your response is a seed you sow. The seed could be a variety of things like when you sow into the lives of others. Sowing into the lives of others could include acts of kindness, giving money or clothing, taking someone shopping, giving an item that solves a problem or supplies a need, etc. When you respond affirmatively, God is setting you up for a harvest. Let me explain what I mean.

The Bible tells us in Psalm 24:1, the earth is the Lord's and the fullness thereof; the world and they that dwell therein[21]. This means everything on planet earth belongs to God, including all the land, resources, wealth, and people. Everything belongs to God, and nothing leaves the earth with us when we die; all the resources, wealth, and materials are his and remain here on earth, and they simply change hands in terms of who possesses them. Therefore, we must all understand that God is the true owner of everything, and we are never owners of anything. Whatever we have in our possession is temporary access, and our possession of those materials makes us stewards or trustees over those materials for a short period. What does this have to do with seedtime and harvest or obedience as a seed, you ask? Well, when God tells you, impresses upon you, or moves on your heart to do something for someone else, like giving something to them, helping them, caring for them, or serving them in some capacity, he is basically telling you to give his stuff or his resources to someone else who needs it now or to use what he has put in your hands in this manner. Your act of obedience to his voice or the leading of his spirit causes two things to happen. First, he is inviting you to participate in his system, and your action is your seed of obedience, and second, he may be rewarding them for some other act/action/seed of obedience they have sown. Either way, this is the process he uses to bless you. Now I know some will say, I don't agree with that or I don't believe that is true, and that's fine. You are entitled to believe whatever you want to believe, but I am simply explaining a law that works for those who choose to work the law.

One final point worth mentioning is the factor of the soil where the seed is sown. In the gospels of Matthew 13, Mark 4, and Luke 8, Jesus tells a parable about a sower who goes out to sow seed. In each account of the parable, the factor that determined the productivity and harvest of the seed was not the seed itself, but rather the soil, the ground, or atmosphere where it was sown. Genesis 1:11-12 tells us that every seed produces after its own kind, but the seed will only produce a harvest if it is sown into GOOD GROUND. If the seed is not sown into the proper soil, it will not produce a harvest. To illustrate this, consider what makes good ground or makes for good soil. Good ground or good soil is that which is conducive for growth. In other words, good ground or good soil contains the necessary nutrients, minerals, and other elements that enable seeds to release their potential in the form of plants, crops, and harvests. According to the parable of the sower, if the seed is not planted, it will be cast to the wayside or be devoured by birds or the enemy. If it is sown among stones, it will not have the ability to develop a root system and will wither away because it doesn't have a sufficient foundation or support system. If the seed is sown among thorns, it will be choked by weeds or suppressed by a hostile environment and not have the ability to produce. The good ground or good soil is the only environment receptive or conducive to the seed and has all the seed needs to release the potential contained within the seed. From a spiritual perspective, good ground could refer to the atmosphere or environment where you live, where you are raised, where you work, where you play, where you socialize, or wherever you might be that brings out your potential. That atmosphere or environment could expose a gift, or an ability to solve problems, create value for others, or do extraordinary things that make you stand out from the crowd to reveal your uniqueness and your value to the world. It will put on display that which makes you necessary in the world and provide a clue to your purpose, assignment, and destiny on the earth. Therefore, the most important point to remember here is that it is not only about the seed sown, but also the soil where it is sown. A seed cannot produce a harvest if it is not sown in the proper atmosphere or proper environment. **NO MATTER WHAT SEED YOU SOW, OR IT'S POTENTIAL, IF IT IS NOT SOWN INTO THE PROPER SOIL (ATMOSPHERE, ENVIRONMENT), IT WILL NOT PRODUCE A HARVEST.** In like manner, if you are not in the right environment necessary for your gifts, talents, skills, abilities, or potential to be released, then you will never release what the world needs that you are carrying inside of you. You must be in the right atmosphere and environment to reveal God's solution in you to serve the world. You and your actions are seeds that are either sown into GOOD GROUND or BAD GROUND.

APPLYING OBEDIENCE AS A SEED

When it comes to applying this principle of obedience as a seed, you must be aware of a biblical principle called Hermeneutics. Hermeneutics is the science or study of biblical interpretation or exegesis. You don't need to go to bible college or seminar, but you need to know a few concepts to correctly apply this concept.

. . .

PRINCIPLE 1. You must know how to interpret scripture, since the scriptures give you the keys, laws, and secrets to the principles of obedience.

HOW TO APPLY PRINCIPLE 1. Interpreting scripture means you must let scripture interpret (explain) scripture. This is important because if you don't know or understand content, context, setting, culture, and a few other elements, you will impose your own understanding of the scripture and not get the proper interpretation. This often happens when people see an apparent "contradiction" in the scripture. They think it is saying one thing, when in truth, it is actually saying something different than what they believe it is saying. In other words, because the person can read, they erroneously believe they can interpret scripture on their own as well as any other book. NOT TRUE. You must find 2-3 scriptures that illustrate the same concept or principle at work. You are looking for what God said, what did the person(s) do, and what was the outcome. You are looking for patterns so that you can interpret and apply the keys/laws/principles correctly. These scriptures will be your foundation for interpretation. If it is a true Bible principle, you will find it consistently in operation throughout scripture, and this will give you confidence that you are on the right track. If you are not sure where to start, look for topics in the scriptures that provide solutions to the areas of your life that have been a challenge for you or where you know you need help to improve. Most Bibles have topics or subjects in the back. Subjects such as finances, business, leadership, relationships, sex, envy, forgiveness, or love are examples of subjects that you can look up. This will begin the process of recalibrating your thinking when it comes to applying the principle of obedience.

PRINCIPLE 2. Pray and ask God to reveal how these scriptures apply to you and show you how to apply them to your own life.

HOW TO APPLY PRINCIPLE 2. Prayer allows you to align your heart and mind to receive illumination from God's spirit about what you prayed for. This step of the process is not to be pious or religious; it is to receive practical instruction from God about how to apply his word to your life. This step is important to understand because two or more people can read the exact same scriptures or set of scriptures but apply them differently according to the uniqueness of their situation or circumstances. You will also want to begin to meditate on the scriptures by thinking, pondering, considering, and mulling over them in your mind what they are saying to you and allowing you to gain understanding about how to apply them to your life.

One of the principles of Hermeneutics is the law of first mention. This means whenever something is mentioned for the first time in scripture; it is establishing a law or foundational principle of doctrine necessary to interpret scripture. One of the laws established in scripture states, "at the mouth of two or three witnesses, let every word be established"[24]. This law or principle is used to establish the credibility of testimony by the mouths of two or three witnesses. In other words, the testimony of one person was insufficient to establish credibility about anything, or against anyone before a judge or in a court of law, unless it could be validated by two or three independent witnesses. This principle of two or three witnesses also means that when God speaks, he will do so two or three times about the same subject matter.

PRINCIPLE 3. You must expect God to speak to you and know how he speaks.

HOW TO APPLY PRINCIPLE 3. God speaks to his people in a still small voice. In other words, he speaks to us in the quiet time of prayer. He will also speak to you through the reading and studying of scripture. He will speak directly into your heart through impressions, and by the peace, he gives you to make a specific decision or move in a certain direction for your life. He will also speak to you through others who don't know you but have a message from him tailored just for your specific situation or circumstance. Sometimes this happens through ministers and preachers in a church setting, other times, it may be someone random off the street or in the local market. What will be undeniable is that God himself wants to get your attention by speaking to those who expect and desire to hear from him.

I want to caution you here to focus on how God speaks and when he is speaking to you and not what his voice sounds like. This may be difficult for some because of how Hollywood has conditioned society to think about what God sounds like. No matter what you believe about God, know that when he does speak, what is being said must line up with scripture. God does this to help you know that it is him. The scriptures give reassurance to the followers that God and his word are one, that he watches over his word to perform it, and that he confirms his word with signs following. Don't focus on if his voice sounds like James Earl Jones, Morgan Freeman, Don LaFontaine, or Hal Douglas. When God speaks, he may be warning you about a certain thing, or you might have a recurring thought that comes to your mind multiple times that won't go away. Sometimes you might hear the same thing repeated from different sources within a short period, sometimes the same day or within the same week. Other times you might read something in scripture, something stated in a magazine, a TV commercial, and hear that point restated multiple times in other places or by multiple people. The point is that when God speaks to you, he will do it multiple times, but no less than two or three times, so you will know he is the one speaking to you. This is one of his patterns for speaking to his messengers and his people. This is also to help you recognize that God is speaking to you to do or not do a thing. For those who are not Bible believers, this principle may be expressed another way. Some would call it having a "gut feeling" or a "hunch" or "intuition" about a thing. Sometimes they may also say something like, "I just had this idea pop into my head" or "something told me I should do/not do a certain." Usually, it takes extraordinary results from the act of obedience before people will realize and recognize that God or "the universe" had something to do with what they heard. Once you know how to interpret scripture and how God speaks, you need to know the fourth Principle.

PRINCIPLE 4. God knows the future, and you and I don't, and he is worthy and deserving to be heard.

HOW TO APPLY PRINCIPLE 4. Understand that God will speak to you personally when you take the time to seek him through prayer by getting quiet long enough to allow him to speak to you. Because he is not limited to the dimensions of time, he knows what will happen and can advise us on the best course of action for any decision we make. This does not mean that it is God's will when we make bad choices or experience negative consequences because we didn't consult with him. God knows what the outcome will be when his laws are obeyed or disobeyed. Our actions lead to predictable outcomes in compliance with or in opposition to his laws. Taking the time to talk to God about what you believe you heard and applying what God spoke to you ensures that we get the best advice, counsel, and results because it's coming from him. Examples of this principle are illustrated in Proverbs 3:5-8, Proverbs 16:1-3, Proverbs 16:9, and Proverbs 19:21.

This is where some people may get upset. God, who created all things, also created you and me for his pleasure and his purpose, not for our own. Therefore, if the creator (God) is speaking to the creation (humanity), it would be prudent to listen, hear, and obey his instructions. He knows the future, and we don't, no matter how hard we try.

Knowing the importance of how and when God speaks is illustrated in Genesis chapter 41, when the pharaoh of Egypt has two dreams that disturb him, which he cannot interpret. A Hebrew slave by the name of Joseph interprets the dreams of Pharaoh, which both foretell of an impending famine to hit Egypt and the surrounding nations. The dream was a warning from God given to Pharaoh twice in the form of dreams. God also gave Joseph a gift of dream interpretation and wisdom that would provide an economic strategy for Egypt to survive and thrive during the famine. The dream and the interpretation created an opportunity for an entirely new economic model for Egypt, and it saved the families of the surrounding nations from famine and preserved the family of Joseph, which today we refer to as the Jewish nation. The interpretation of the dream and obedience to the wisdom of God caused Joseph to be elevated from being a slave in Egypt to Prime Minister of Egypt and second in command over the nation second only to Pharaoh. It also created a wealth transference from all the surrounding nations into the hands of Egypt, making it the most powerful nation in the known world at that time.

In Pharaoh's dream, he saw the famine in two different forms, but he didn't know the meaning of the dreams, nor did he realize that God was speaking to him through the dream. If Joseph had not been in Pharaoh's kingdom to interpret the dream, Egypt and the known nations of the world at the time would have perished because no one would have known that God was speaking or how he spoke. This story not only expresses the importance of recognizing God's voice and how he speaks, but it also illustrates the importance of knowing the value of your gift and how to use it. The lives of others may depend on it. Once you have identified that God is speaking to you, it becomes necessary to choose to obey God's instructions.

PRINCIPLE 5. You must choose to obey God.

HOW TO APPLY PRINCIPLE 5. To obey God once you know He is speaking to you requires trust, confidence, and being fully persuaded, aka faith. You already know that He speaks in-line with what scripture says. You know he speaks in the mouth of two or three witnesses. You already know he will speak in a still small voice in your prayer time. You also know he will speak in your heart directly to you. So now the only thing that is stopping you from obeying him is fear, fear of the unknown, fear of missing it or making a mistake. The beautiful thing about choosing to obey God, or acting in faith, is that hopefully, your focus or goal is to please him or do his will. There are two to three main points of faith: to please God, to do the will of God, and to obey God.

Here is a word of encouragement for anyone attempting to please God or do the will of God. He would never tell you to do something that you cannot do. Second, he will not tell you to do something that does not please Him. Third, he will not tell you to do something that goes against his will. For example, Hebrews 11:6 states, "but without faith, it is impossible to please him: for he that comes to God must believe that He is, and that He is a rewarder of them that diligently seek Him." This scripture says that without faith, it is impossible to please God, and when we go to God, we must believe that God is all that He says he is in His word. Hebrews 11:7-40, gives us examples of people in the Bible who lived by faith and obeyed God. These scriptures give a glimpse of how we please God.

This point will probably anger some people because many in today's culture either don't believe in God, don't believe God speaks to people today, or don't want anyone telling them what they should or should not be doing in their lives. This is maybe because some people have had negative experiences in their lives when it comes to the subject of God, the Bible, the Church, religion, or anything else remotely related. The intent of this book is not to address the subject of Church or religion, but it is intended to make you aware of some spiritual laws that God created that could be affecting some areas of your life based on some of your actions.

Principle 6. You must discern God's timing and if you are to act immediately or wait for other instructions. When God gives instruction for you to obey, does He always speak 2-3 times?

How to apply Principle 6. You must ask God when you are to act on his instructions. There are moments where waiting to do a thing is necessary because other elements, people, events may need to be in alignment for things to connect and work together smoothly according to God's plan and purpose. Sometimes, people call this serendipity where things coincidentally come together as if they were planned. They were.

Another point to consider is, if God only gives a partial instruction, then you may need to wait for Him to reveal more. For example, if He told you to do something for someone, you may need to know who to do it for, when, and how. If God instructed you to move to another geographic location, waiting for further instruction would be wise to have direction rather than creating chaos out of being impatient.

PRINCIPLE 7. Complete every instruction God gives so that you are not operating in partial obedience, or delayed obedience.

HOW TO APPLY PRINCIPLE 7. Write down any instructions you have received from God. Check to make sure the instructions line up (agree with/harmonize) with God's word. Mark off each instruction one by one until every instruction is completed. Total obedience to God's instructions authorizes him to move on your behalf and bless you as he promised. God's word promises if we are willing and obedient, we will eat of the good of the land. It also promises that only the doer of the work is blessed. Your obedience is the only proof that you have that demonstrates you expect God to keep his word to you. So remember, you must obey him completely by completing every instruction.

There is nothing worse for you when you are expecting God to move in your life than for you to only do a portion of what he said to do or to delay in your obedience. The partial obedience you sow creates the partial opportunities you reap. The delayed obedience you sow produces the delayed or missed reward you reap. Both instances are called disobedience. Disobedience never pleases God, never fulfills his will, and it will not persuade him to move on your behalf. Faith pleases God, and obedience is an act of faith. As we conclude this section, always remember that when God speaks, he will speak at least two to three times to let you know that it is him. Follow that instruction or set of instructions immediately to the best of your ability, and you will be reaping a reward or harvest from your seed of obedience.

3
TIME AS A SEED

Psalm 90:10 states in part: The days of our years are threescore years and ten; and if by reason of strength, they are fourscore years. It goes on in verse 12 and states: So teach us to number our days, that we may apply our hearts unto wisdom. Matthew 6:20 states: For where your treasure is, there will your heart be also. These scriptures, when put together, paint a picture of the importance and value of our time. They also reveal a few vital points we should be aware of, such as: time is finite and should never be wasted. Second, they reveal that our time on earth is limited and granted to us by God. Third, they reveal that whatever is valuable to us, we will spend, use up, or invest our time into. In other words, the usage of our time demonstrates what we value and what we will exchange our time for. This is what we do with our finances and other resources. We will exchange our money for what we want, and likewise, we will exchange our time for what we value. Like money, there are at least three things we can do with our time: waste it, spend it, or invest it. In other words, time and money are mediums of exchange or types of currency we use to exchange for what we want or value. Money is the currency used to exchange for things we want or need. Time is a type of currency used as a medium of exchange for what we value, but the difference between time and money is that there is an endless supply of money on earth, but there is a limited amount of time given to each of us to be on planet earth. Our time is in limited supply, and we only have enough of it to accomplish all that we're designed and created to accomplish. The time we have can be used as seeds to grow and produce the harvest we want, need, and were created to produce, or they can be used to create a life full of regret, unwanted consequences, or unintended results. It is for this reason that I am identifying time as a seed. Remember, the law of seedtime and harvest is always at work whenever we sow our seed(s). If we intentionally begin to use our time as a seed, it will produce a harvest or a series of harvests necessary to accomplish great things in our lives. Time is a distinct and precious seed because everyone was given life to fulfill their purpose on earth, which requires utilizing their allotment of time. Some people, however, treat their time as unwanted pennies, nickels, and dimes, which some throw away or allow to drop to the ground never to be picked up, reclaimed, or used by them again. I realize that some people prefer the kind of money that can be folded over than that which jingles, but all forms and denominations of money are useful, and both time and money can be wasted, spent, or invested. If we manage the change that jingles in our pockets, we will be able to handle the paper that folds even better. The same is also true with our time; when we manage our time-based activities better, we will produce much better results in our lives with it and have more time to do more meaningful things. A popular saying that businesspeople use frequently is that TIME IS MONEY. This statement is accurate concerning business, but I want to correct that notion. Time is not MONEY, but time is PRECIOUS. When we begin to recognize that time is precious, we can begin to be intentional and make positive, conscious decisions with our time and sow it into activities and endeavors worthy of the most precious of all seeds; our time.

There is a rule regarding the time that many peak performers live by and promote to their fans, followers, and admirers; it's called the 10,000-Hour Rule (Gladwell, November 18, 2008). This rule states that to become an expert or a master at anything or in any field, you must invest at least 10,000 concentrated hours of focused activity into that area. It is through this process of practice, repetition, correction, and repeating that a person eventually becomes an expert or a master in their field. When this 10,000-Hour Rule is understood and applied, those that do so usually implement it in their lives immediately over three to five years to get to the mastery stage quickly. This is the amount of time necessary for anyone to immerse themselves into an activity or endeavor to become an expert or to achieve mastery the fastest. This time of immersive development requires total commitment, laser focus, obsession, being relentless and unstoppable to become the best at what you do. There is a measure of truth to this 10,000-Hour Rule.

When you see those at the top of their field or career in any industry, most of them, if not all, have invested the time, they've practiced, they've worked, and now are reaping the rewards for all they have all sacrificed to achieve. Often, they've had to forfeit other desires or interests to achieve their current objectives. Sometimes, family, friends, or other relationships were put on the backburner temporarily to pursue this higher station or calling in life. Their time was being utilized as a seed to produce a harvest they may reap for many years to come. I don't want this point to be missed, so I will repeat it: Sometimes, family, friends, or other relationships were put on the backburner temporarily to pursue this higher station or calling in life and their time was being utilized as a seed to produce a harvest they may reap for many years to come. This is not to suggest that personal relationships like having a spouse or children are unimportant, but any relationship that does not help you to achieve your purpose in life might be a relationship worth sacrificing. In fact, I believe that the best definition of a friend is anyone who helps you to reach your destiny or fulfill your mission in life. Some people have invested their time to become the best of the best in their industry by being ALL IN or being totally committed to their craft, career, and industry. When you hear certain people's names mentioned, their names are usually synonymous with what they do. These individuals have achieved a level of success and excellence in their industries that has raised the bar for others and have set new standards for greatness, excellence, and success.

These individuals are known by one name, usually their first or last name, or by their initials. For example, in the sports arena, you recognize names like Jordan, James, Tiger, Serena, Beckham, Rice, and Brady, to name a few. In the music industry, it might be names like Prince, Elvis, Perry, Swift, Tupac, Beyoncé, or Jay-Z. In film, names like De Niro, Pacino, Streep, or Denzel come to mind. In the world of business or technology, names like Gates, Buffet, Jobs, Bezos, Trump, or Zuckerberg might ring a bell. In politics, names like Carter, Clinton, Bush, or Obama come to mind. For television, one name stands out in this generation; Oprah! For ministry, names like Graham, Roberts, Jakes, and Copeland, ring out. Whether you like or agree with any of those persons mentioned here, the point is clear; these individuals have made their marks in their industries or sphere of influence and have invested their time, energy, and their abilities, and they are excelling. These individuals are examples of the 10,000 Hour-Rule, and they are not just good at what they do, they are what they do; they are masters of their craft and leaders in their industry and sphere of influence. Through the investment of their time and development of skill, some have become household names and have transitioned into becoming commercial brands, meaning not only are they popular among their fans, followers, and admirers, but they have also found financial success with products bearing their name. This is also an important point to understand: when you are excellent or the best at what you do, not only does your name become great, but your name begins to have monetary value.

Your name becomes a company brand or a household name that may produce, provide, and promote products, goods, and services that consumers will purchase. This market of consumers wants to wear your name or your brand on their feet, on their heads, on their backs, on their wrists, or other parts of their bodies. This is called branding in the business world. The discipline, diligence, and excellence exhibited by these masters in their industries convey a monetary value in the marketplace. It means your name or brand communicates a certain value or standard that others are attracted to, believe in, identify with, and will spend money on. It also means other companies recognize and respect your brand and are willing to invest millions of dollars in endorsement deals to get you to promote their products, goods, and services using that brand. This all goes back to the importance of your time being sown as a seed. Not only does this apply in the world of sports and entertainment, but it also applies in other areas as well.

When you think of world changers, you think of people like Nelson Mandela, Dr. Martin Luther King Jr., Mahatma Gandhi, and Mother Theresa. When you think of history makers, other names come to mind like Adolf Hitler, Joseph Stalin, Benito Mussolini, Osama Bin Laden, and others. Those listed above used their time, talent, abilities, passions, personalities, and resources to create movements, change cultures, affect public policies, wreak havoc upon the world, or challenged the status quo. Whether you love and admire them, or whether you despise and loathe them, these are names forever etched into the history books, and the social fabric of society and their memory and legacies can never be erased. The world will never be the same because they left their mark on the world. Some sowed their time to make the world a better place, whereas others sowed their time destroying humanity.

APPLYING TIME AS A SEED

When it comes to applying your time as a seed, a few questions to ask yourself might include: How am I using my time right now? Am I wasting, spending, or investing my time into things that matter or have no value at all? How are my actions today going to affect future generations? Will I be remembered for what I am doing right now? Will I be remembered when I'm gone? How will I be remembered when I'm gone? Will my actions today be remembered 100 hundred years from now? Will there be anything that will document my life, my memory, or my contribution to the human family? How long will my name live on beyond my life? These are the kinds of questions that kings, emperors, and royalty are obsessed with because they want their names to live on for infinity. This is referred to as their legacy or their glory. Your glory or legacy is what people talk about or remember you for, that made you unforgettable. These are also the kinds of question people ask who desire to be significant, who desire to be great, who want their lives to matter, who want to make an impact on the world, who want to feel important, who want to feel special, who want to feel valuable, or who want to feel unique. These questions force you to go deep within and search your own heart for your true motives or your WHY for being or to pursue God for the meaning of your life.

PRINCIPLE 1. Ask God what is your purpose and how you should use your time?

HOW TO APPLY PRINCIPLE 1. You can pray according to

Proverbs 3:5-8; Proverbs 16:3; James 1:1-7. For example, a prayer could be, "Father, I trust you with all my heart; I lean not to my own understanding, but I acknowledge you concerning my purpose, and I ask you to direct my path (Proverbs 3:5-6). Father, I commit my purpose to you and ask you to establish my thoughts (Proverbs 16:3). Father, I ask you to reveal to me what you have created me to do (knowledge), what problem I was created to solve (gifting), why is it important (understanding), and how to accomplish my purpose (assignment) and how to apply my purpose to my life everyday (wisdom)."

Keep in mind you must believe God heard your prayer, He answered your prayer, and is revealing your purpose to you, and you must hold on to this no matter what and no matter how long it takes. This is important because, according to God's word, those who waver should not think he or she shall receive anything of the Lord because he or she is double-minded and unstable in all his ways. Seek the Lord through prayer to get his guidance, counsel, and direction. Your purpose is the reason why you exist and what you were born to do. The importance of this single point cannot be overstated. There are multitudes of people who live and die, never discovering their purpose in life or engage in many alternative activities wasting their time and end up settling for the pursuit of fame, fortune, power, happiness, or comfort rather than pursuing purpose. The pursuit of purpose is the only thing that will truly bring fulfillment in life, and there are no other substitutions for it. The pursuit of wealth, fame, or power in and of themselves only cannot compare to the pursuit and fulfillment of purpose. Fame, fortune, or power might come with the pursuit, but should not be the focus of one's pursuit in life. The pursuit for purpose is closely linked to your pursuit of God. This is important to understand because God is the creator of every person on earth, and he placed every gift, talent, and ability you possess within you. Those abilities and capacities are clues to help you discover, identify, and fulfill your purpose. Now people can use these abilities to have a comfortable life. Many have used their abilities to pursue fame, fortune, and power, but end up miserable, unhappy, unfulfilled, and never fulfilled their purpose, simply because they never took the time to consult with God.

Principle 2. Write out a plan of action to pursue your purpose (S.M.A.R.T Goal)

How to apply Principle 2. Your plan of action should be S.M.A.R.T. (Specific, Measurable, Attainable, Relevant, Time-Bound). This is necessary to help keep you on track with what you are doing with your time and your life. Our timetable is not the same as God's but, writing out a plan gives you and God something to work with. Your purpose plan should include what, why, how, when, where, with whom, etc. Fill in all these parts as best as you can to help you create a plan. For example, if God revealed to you that part of your purpose was to start and run a school, then continue to seek him about what type of school to start and what kind of curriculum, why start a school, how to create it and what method to use to run the school, where will the school be located, who do you need to help you, is there anyone to partner with, who are the students, etc. To the best of your ability, capture as much detail as you can as he gives it so that not only will you have it in writing, but you can refer back to it as often as is necessary.

This is an action plan, something you can start today to get you started. Make sure your action plans have activities that are practical, measurable, and have a deadline. Without these elements, your plan might be too vague, lacking a specific target with no way of tracking your progress or determining your level of productivity or success.

PRINCIPLE 3. Be highly selective of who you allow into your life and have access to your time.

HOW TO APPLY PRINCIPLE 3. Ask yourself if the people in your life are adding to your life, multiplying your life, subtracting from your life, or dividing from your life. In other words, while you are pursuing your goals, make sure the people who have access to you, qualify to have access to your time. This means they must add value to your life, you are adding value to theirs, or there is a mutual exchange of value. Make every waking moment of your life an opportunity to focus on doing something that enables your purpose to come forth and be expressed.

All the relationships you have should add value to your life, but you just have to discern what that value is in light of your purpose. There are several categories of relationships that develop in your life. Some of these relationships include family, friends, foes, cheerleaders, mentors, peers, and proteges. Family is those you are connected to you by blood, marriage, or adoption. These are the people you have little say-so regarding their connection to you. They are there to help you learn how to deal with or handle people in life because each one is different and has its own set of behaviors and challenges. The second group is your friends. These are the people you selected and allowed to be in your life. They love you just the way you are and are there because you let them in. The third group is the foes. These are those who oppose you because of your purpose, assignment, decisions, or relationships. Your life upsets them, challenges them, or provokes them to oppose you. They may not even know why they oppose you, but they are necessary for your learning, growth, and development. They are a sign that promotion is on the way based on how you handle them or an indication of areas you still need to grow. The fourth group is your cheerleaders. These are those who cheer you on or encourage you to keep on going when you feel unsure about yourself. These people want to see you win in life. You are their motivation, and in turn, they provide you with motivation. The fifth group is mentors. These are those who are there to help you win but are not interested in your feelings, past accomplishments, ego, or anything else, except you winning. They push you to push past your feelings and insecurities, and jerk the slack out of you when you are being lazy or doing less than your best. They love you too much to let you stay the way you were when they met you. They will always tell you what you need to hear and not what you want to hear and might not say it so nicely. In fact, some mentors can be downright mean or rude and will hurt your feelings, but they are one of the fastest ways to help you get to your destiny and reach your goals. They are tried, battle-tested, and proven in their sphere of influence. They have been there, done that. They bought the hat, T-shirt, sunglasses, belt, and the shoes, and they know what it takes to get where you are going. The next group is your peers. These are those who are in your industry, they do what you do, they may or may not be your age, have a similar background, or are on a similar journey as yours and want to see you win. They face similar challenges as you but also face different obstacles that you can glean wisdom from and vice-versa. They want the best for you, and hopefully, you want the best for them. The last group is the proteges. These are those who you mentor, who look up to you and seek you out for guidance, counsel, wisdom, or help in some area of life. They want to be where you are, have what you have, do what you do, or even want to replace you. All of these relationships, however, are necessary for you, and there should be a mutual exchange for the value you offer to each other. This is not to suggest that you cannot enjoy your life pursuing your purpose, but it does mean assessing the value of these relationships is vital for helping you know who is necessary for your life and who is not. This is important because people who are going nowhere want you to go nowhere with them, and if they do not value their own time, they will not value yours. One side note; if they don't value their own time, they will, in many cases, be wasters of money or other valuable resources as well.

Principle 4. Surround yourself with others who are purpose-driven and who have a sense of focus and destiny in their lives.

How to apply Principle 4. Consider obtaining one-on-coaching, joining a think-tank, or becoming a member of a mastermind group. Seek out and connect with individuals and groups who are disciplined, self-starters, highly motivated, have a laser-sharp focus on determining their values, proficient in goal setting, time management, and are solution-oriented.

These options place you in environments that will challenge you, provoke innovative thinking, advance new ideas, and create synergy for new opportunities, collaborations, joint ventures, and partnerships. You also want to be among those who are making history by expressing their purpose through the vehicles of new companies, organizations, and institutions. This principle also suggests that you are a reflection of the company you keep. Therefore new, higher, and better ideas require new, higher, and better thinking, and sometimes it will require agreement with those who dispense new ideas. The scriptures give a warning that two cannot walk together unless they agree.

Principle 5. Be discriminating in whom you receive and accept advice, counsel, and input from.

How to apply Principle 5. When soliciting advice, counsel, or input, ask yourself the following questions: Are they qualified to give you the counsel they are offering? What do they do, and how long have they been at it? Do they live by the counsel they give? What is the fruit in their own lives from the advice they are offering? Is their counsel sound, proven, and worthy of acceptance? Do they have a documented track record of successfully helping others? What success stories do they have? Whom have they mentored?

These are just a few questions you can use to pre-qualify and use as a vetting process for would-be armchair advisors regarding their counsel and advice to you. If you never forget these principles, you will save yourself from headaches, heartaches, disappointments, and frustration. The fundamental principle here is: God is not mocked for whatsoever a man sows, that shall he also reap[30]. Whenever you help others, it will come back around to you like clockwork, and the help you receive will always be greater than the help you gave. Remember, seedtime and harvest is a law. This means it will work for anyone, anywhere around the world. Your time is never wasted if you are intentional with sowing your time as opposed to spending or wasting it.

4

FAITH AS A SEED

In this section, I want to address the subject of Faith being a seed. As stated earlier, seedtime and harvest is a law that will work anywhere, anytime, for anyone. Faith is also a seed that will work for anyone, anywhere, anytime. The Bible teaches in Romans 10:17: So then faith comes by hearing, and hearing by the word of God. You must hear the word of God to have faith. Faith does not come by reading; it comes by hearing. When you hear the word of God, you are hearing the promises and principles of God being spoken, taught, or preached, and faith from those principles and promises comes off the page into your heart. Also, faith doesn't just come into your heart by hearing the word, but faith grows every time you hear those same thoughts, ideas, principles, or laws spoken, taught, or preached. In other words, you reinforce and strengthen your faith based on what you heard, causing it to become solidified in your heart. A simple definition of faith is trust, confidence, or persuasion in God, his principles, and his promises. Human Faith is simply ACTING ON WHAT YOU BELIEVE. Bible faith is ACTING ON THE WRITTEN OR SPOKEN WORD OF GOD. The reason why this is important to know and understand is that when you hear people speak about their dreams, goals, or plans, many times, they are speaking of their own faith or human faith. They might not be operating in Bible faith, which is centered and focused on doing the will of God or doing that which pleases God. Why is this important, you ask? Whenever someone has placed themselves in the center of what they are doing or intend to do, it usually has nothing to do with God or his will. How then can you know the difference between human faith and Bible faith? Human faith always seeks what best for the unholy trinity: Me, Myself, and I. Human faith is always self-serving and focuses on doing what makes them happy, and seldom seeks to do the will of God or that which is for the well-being of others. Bible faith, on the other hand, seeks to do the will of God, which is counter-intuitive to our natural inclinations. Bible faith also seeks to fulfill the will of God on earth, and many times it will affect or benefit others. Human faith does sometimes produce tangible results in the lives of those individuals who are resolved to see their goals, dreams, and desires come to pass.

In some cases, their efforts pay-off handsomely and affect the lives of others. The achieved results become the foundation that justifies for them why they do what they do, despite what scripture teaches. In other words, some people have the mentality that if what they're doing and how they're living gets them the results they want, why would they or why should they change?

This mentality will help you understand the definition of human faith given above, acting on what you believe. The problem here, however, is that the individual rarely considers if God is pleased or if God's will is accomplished. Remember, Bible faith always seeks to do or fulfill the will of God on earth. This is what Jesus did as well as all of those who are recorded in scripture. Sometimes doing the will of God goes against everything in you or is contrary to your personal views and opinions. But here are a few questions that must be addressed to assess if you are operating in human faith or bible faith. How did this effort or activity accomplish or fulfill the will of God? Is there a biblical foundation for the result achieved? What results were achieved? How many people have been affected, and on what scale were the results attained? These become challenging questions to answer for some because, at the end of the day, the issue becomes who gets the credit for all that was achieved? Scripture declares that God will not share his glory (praise/credit) with anyone, so consider this; if the individual gets the attention and credit, then all the effort, attention, and accolades were all about the individual. If, however, God gets the attention and credit, then it was all about God. When an activity or endeavor is ordained by God, it will always point to him in some way, have the potential to reach a wider or global audience, and demonstrate his ability (potential, power, or authority), operating in and through the person acting in faith. This is important to understand because it takes bible faith to pursue, engage in, and accomplish the will of God. You would have to have trust, confidence in and be fully persuaded by God and his word to do something that he ordains or commands that goes against anything and everything you what to do. Your faith must be based on the known will of God if you are going to act. One thing, however, that can be confusing to some is whether a non-Christian can fulfill the will of God. This can be confusing because if the person does not believe in God, how can that person fulfill the will of God? Obviously, this creates theological problems to answer for some. The scripture does offer this piece of wisdom; it states in Proverbs 16:4 (MSG Translations), GOD made everything with a place and purpose; even the wicked are included—but for *judgment*. Suffice it to say that, if the end result points to God in some way, has the potential to reach the masses and puts God's ability to display operating through the individual, it could be said that the person was doing the will of God even though he or she might not know anything about Bible faith or the will of God.

The Bible states in Hebrews 11:1 that faith is the substance of things hoped for, the evidence of things, not seen. According to this verse of scripture, faith has the substance that can be hoped for and has evidence that is not seen. What has the substance that can be hoped for? A vision, a goal, a plan of action. All of these things are some kind of substance that can be hoped for, and hopefully, it came from God. What kind of evidence cannot be seen? A dream, a desire, or something created by the imagination that cannot be seen by the naked eye. It has evidence because it can only be seen by the person who can see the invisible, and this gives them the ability to do the impossible because they believe it is possible. Whenever a person is in faith, they speak based on what they believe is real, what they believe is true, or what they believe is possible even when others cannot or do not see it or believe it themselves. I am not referring to a person that may have a mental illness, delusional, be under the influence of drugs, or not rooted in reality. I am referring to a person who is in faith (seeking to do the will of God) and speaks as if something already is a reality. When they speak, they see the future as being right here, right now, and in the present. It is because of this worldview or perspective that these kinds of people seem a little out of touch with "reality." These are also the same people who, when they bring their visions to pass, are recognized as geniuses, pioneers, innovators, and those ahead of their time. Think of the people who had ideas so far-fetched that no one believed in them until they made the impossible possible. People like Ray Croc developer of the franchise model for McDonalds, Sam Walton founder of Walmart and Sam's Club, Bill Gates founder of Microsoft, Steve Jobs founder of Apple Inc., Jeff Bezos, founder and CEO of Amazon, Elon Musk founder of Space-X, Tesla Inc, co-founder of Neuralink, and co-founder of PayPal, and Jack Ma, founder of Alibaba are all examples of people who saw the invisible and have done what was considered impossible.

APPLYING FAITH AS A SEED

Principle 1. Acting in faith begins where the will of God is known.

How to apply Principle 1. Begin reading the word of God daily for information and listening to sound biblical teaching from God's word for inspiration to build your faith. Also, develop a regularly scheduled time of studying scripture to recalibrate your thinking to be in line with God's word.

For some, these steps may seem tedious or cumbersome; however, all of these activities are part of the process of developing a spiritual life and necessary to develop your faith. Remember, you are interested in God moving in your life and want the kind of results that only God's word can produce. You are not interested in being tied to a system that man controls and can manipulate. God's system is full proof and works all the time, anywhere, and for anyone who will trust him and put his word to work in their own lives. As you dig into the scriptures, these steps will help you develop a sound foundation so that you will know what God's best is for your life in all areas. This process will also aid you in knowing God's heart concerning mankind and his creation. This process is not about being overly religious, pious, or super-spiritual, but it is about learning how to tap into the unlimited power, authority, and ability of God that can be released into and transform your life. As you go on this journey, you will know why faith is important and how to apply it to your life. Once God's will is established in your heart, the seed of faith will be able to be planted.

If you do not know the will of God, how can you fulfill it? You may know your own will regarding how you want to live your life and use your time, talents, and your abilities. But if you did not create yourself, bestow your gifts, talents, and abilities upon yourself, how then can you be certain that your will and the will of your creator are the same? This is an example of human faith, bringing your own will, goals, or desires to pass. Now I realize with everything that has been stated in this book up to this point assumes that you, the reader, already believe in God, accept God as being real and that you and I are accountable to Him for how we live our lives. If this assumption is incorrect about you, then there are only three ways for you to know if what is stated here about God's existence, God's word, and God's will are true. The first way is to act in obedience based on God's word to experience what happens on the other side of your obedience. The second way is to disobey God's word to see what happens now that you know a little bit about his system. The third way is to die. WOW, pretty extreme, huh? Pretty narrow-minded, you might say. After death, you will know for sure whether God exists or whether there is or was a "will of God" for you to fulfill. I realize these are some blunt statements and may possibly offend some of you who read this. You may believe that I am pronouncing some form of judgment or a curse upon you. This is not the case at all, but hearing the truth, facing your own mortality, and facing death has a way of sobering you to some very real and permanent realities.

If I made similar statements about the possibility of you or a loved one going to prison for life or an extended period of time for some criminal offense you or your loved one committed, were arrested for, tried and sentenced, that would not seem so farfetched to you because you have a point of reference for that. But if you bring up this very real subject, one's mortality and accountability to God for how you and I lived, suddenly it is considered rude, offensive, primitive, narrow-minded, hate speech, or being judgmental. You and I know that people go to prison every day for crimes they were convicted of, and most of us believe that they probably deserved being locked up. But if it doesn't affect us or someone personally we know, then it is out of sight and out of mind. We also tend to think of ourselves as good people who deserve good things coming our way. If God is not real to you, you have nothing to worry about, and truthfully you ought not even to be offended by these statements about your mortality, hell, or even an afterlife affecting you. If, however, you believe in your heart that there is potentially a day of judgment for our actions, where God judges how we lived our lives and whether we accomplished or pursued his will for our lives, then maybe there is something here you need to seriously consider. If these statements about God being real and all the scriptures say is true, you now have a decision to make whether you will choose to believe and accept the truth, or to continue living as you have up to this point and until you take your final breath. The will of God is documented in a manual for humanity called the Bible. If you read it, hear it, and study it, you will have an opportunity to discover God's will for your life. When you know and are clear on God's will for your life, you will have developed trust and confidence in God and his word, which creates within you a paradigm shift. You will view the world and what is possible through a different worldview.

PRINCIPLE 2. Activate God's promises in your life by speaking his promises over your life daily.

HOW TO APPLY PRINCIPLE 2. Daily confess the promises of God over your life that you discover in the scriptures. As you grow in knowledge, understanding, and wisdom, claim God's promises as your own, and pray and ask Him to reveal His will to you and expect that He will do it. As God reveals His will to you, speak it and meditate on God's will regularly until you act on it confidently. When you know God's will for your life, and it is established in your heart, you will begin to speak it (Luke 6:45).

You will know that this has occurred because what you believe about God and his word will affect your speech. This is important to know because faith always speaks what it believes. In other words, you will begin speaking about what you want God to do in your life or situation, what you believe He can do, or what you expect to happen as if it will happen or you will speak as if it has already happened. This expresses an attitude of expectation that means that faith is now in your heart.

PRINCIPLE 3. Take action on what you believe based on the written and spoken word of God.

HOW TO APPLY PRINCIPLE 3. Begin taking steps of faith by acting/implementing God's principles in the areas of your life you want to see God move. You will do things that agree with your faith and the will of God. Act boldly and confidently, knowing that God loves you and wants the best for you.

BY ACTING on the word of God or by acting in obedience to the word of God, you are acting in faith. Faith requires taking action because faith is not thinking, hoping, or believing. To believe means to accept something as being true or being the truth; however, believing alone is not faith. When you take action, you demonstrate what you believe, you are demonstrating faith, and you are applying faith as a seed. In this regard, you are applying faith as a seed to fulfill His will for your life. If you simply act on what you believe contrary to the word of God, you are operating in human faith. Human faith can and often does produce some tangible results in your life, but it rarely will accomplish God's will for your life. Remember, faith is the substance of things hoped for and the evidence of things not seen. As you seek to accomplish your goals, dreams, desires, and plans, ask yourself who will get the credit or the glory: me, or God? That question will always help you to locate your own heart and your own motives and whether your actions or in faith or not.

5

THOUGHTS AS A SEED

The next concept I want to introduce to you, the reader, is the concept of your idea or ideas being seeds. This concept is one of the most powerful on earth because everyone has thoughts and ideas running through their minds daily. Everyone on planet earth has thoughts and ideas that govern how they make decisions and how they live their lives. Thoughts are ideas, concepts, or words in pictures. A thought is a picture or something you can see in your mind. Your thoughts are also the seeds that can germinate in your mind. The late Dr. Myles E. Munroe stated that the world is ruled by dead men. In other words, the thoughts, ideas, and concepts of dead men are shaping, influencing, and ruling the world we live in. When you consider the ideas, concepts, and philosophy of politics, democracy, capitalism, socialism, religion, or anything else that informs, influences, or shapes cultural thinking or belief, it is undeniable of the impact that dead men's ideas have on the world. They are still here with us and have been used to create systems, cycles, processes, companies, and nations. A thought is an image in the mind, and the ability to create or produce these images is sometimes called imagination. Your imagination can conjure up many images and stir up your emotions.

Psychology, which is the study of the human mind, its functions, and human behavior, teaches that the mind cannot distinguish between a real event and an imagined event. To prove this point, think back to the last dream or nightmare you had or simply recall any negative or traumatic experience that had your full attention. Whatever you were thinking about, dreaming about or imagined seemed so real to you that when you woke up, your emotions were stirred-up, your heart was pounding, and your breathing intensified. You realized it was all a dream, yet your emotions were agitated. You may have been happy, angry, scared, aroused, or excited at that moment, and as a result, you had an emotion that created an experience that created a memory that remained with you until this very day. This is especially true if the dream or nightmare is connected to an actual event you experienced. If you experienced something traumatic, it might have embedded itself into your subconscious mind causing you to experience nightmares or night terrors. Every time you think about or recall the memory is like reliving the experience all over again, and your mind cannot distinguish it as being the past. In reality, you may know the experience is in the past, but in your dream and emotions, you may not have gotten over the experience, and it could still possibly be affecting your life today. This is because it was all in your subconscious mind.

Your mind, your memories, and your experiences go with you everywhere you go, so they are always with you. Many times, your emotions cannot distinguish between a real thing and an imagined thing, especially if the event was traumatic, and you never got closure. As far as the mind is concerned, it is all the same, and it is still very real to you. Think about any experience that made you mad and how you felt about that experience. Think about the happiest moments you've experienced in your life. Those memories caused you to experience those same intense emotions all over again as if it just happened. This is because every memory we have has an emotion attached to it, and our minds assign a value to it based on how it made us feel. You are taken back to the details of the event, and your senses are fully engaged. In your mind and emotions, you are still there. This is based on the principle of meditation.

I am not speaking of the kind of meditation that is practiced in eastern religions where you clear your mind of any thoughts, but I am referring to the practice or habit of rolling things over in your mind repeatedly. I am referring to the practice of muttering, pondering, considering, and mulling over the ideas, concepts, or memories in your mind, over and over again. When you meditate, you are thinking deeply or intensely about something, and maybe your mind is attempting to resolve the issue or is seeking for a solution to the issue. In that light, here is a principle for your consideration: whatever you focus on grows in your mind and in your life. Here is another idea: your feelings or emotions follow your focus. What this means is whatever you are thinking about deeply or intensely has the potential to intensify in your mind and intensify your feelings or emotions about that thing. If your thoughts are fruitful and solution-oriented, this can be an incredibly useful and productive use of imagination and creativity. Your thoughts can be utilized to be inventive, creating new technologies, innovative strategies for producing and doing things better, faster, and more efficiently. Your concentrated thoughts may discover solutions to age-old problems, creating new companies, organizations, or new industries affecting public policies, cultures, and economies. On the flip side, if your thoughts are critical, pessimistic, or negative, this can be detrimental and incredibly dangerous because you are not seeking solutions or seeking to resolve the issue. You are looking for logical reasons to justify your negative thoughts and why things went wrong or why you deserved what happened to you.

A self-centered perspective could influence you to become an instrument of destruction rather than a beacon of light and hope for others. For example, if you are sad, lonely, depressed, feeling unloved, unappreciated, or some other negative emotion, those thoughts can lead you down a path that can be harmful to yourself or to others. It is often discovered that those who have engaged in mass shootings in public spaces frequently experience these kinds of emotions, which influences them to behave in this destructive manner. The mind is always seeking ways to help itself or protect itself from anyone or anything perceived as a threat. Mental illness is not the focus of this book but suffice it to say that part of the neurological and chemical imbalance in the brain that these individuals experience plays a significant role in influencing the emotions and decision-making ability of these individuals. Those thoughts have influenced some to commit heinous crimes, or other evil acts against others or even against themselves. Those thoughts were seeds that germinated in the hearts and minds of individuals who may not have had a strong and solid spiritual or family support system. In their minds, they simply want the loss, pain, or suffering to end by any means necessary. Whatever a person meditates on consistently or for long periods eventually grows in their lives. At that point, it is simply a matter of when and not if they act on those negative thoughts.

HERE IS A NUGGET OF WISDOM: DECISIONS LEAD TO YOUR DESTINY, BUT NOT EVERY DECISION IS ORDAINED BY GOD.

This is a very important point to consider. Your decision can lead down a path that, if continued upon, will lead to a certain destiny or destination. Our decisions are our decisions no matter what happens in life, but every decision we make, however, is not necessarily ordained by God. Many people believe that everything that happens in life is Gods' will or his doing even when or especially when something bad or evil happens. One important variable to consider, however, is the input that we solicit from God or others. Prov. 3:5-6 states: Trust in the Lord with all thine heart, and lean not unto thy own understanding. In all thy ways, acknowledge him, and he shall direct thy path[34]. This means if we seek God or acknowledge God in our decision making, we can be assured that he will direct our path. If we follow the counsel of those who are unwise, or if we simply follow our own desires, things might not turn out the way we plan. This is based on Prov. 14:12, which states: There is a way which seemeth right unto a man, but the end thereof are the ways of death. This is not saying you are incapable of making wise decisions; however, making decisions without wise counsel or not seeking God could prove to be detrimental to your own life. Gods' intention for our lives is good and not evil. It is intended to give us peace and an expected end (Jeremiah 29:11). However, our decisions in life can alter our destiny. In other words, nothing just happens. Nothing good or evil just happens. There is always a cause, even if we are ignorant about the cause. Our decisions can also alter the route or the process of development we must go through to be made ready or fit for our purpose. Some believe that God is not wasteful with our experiences and that a detour in our lives is not necessarily a bad thing or a denial of development for our purpose. For example, Romans 8:28 states: And we know all things work together for our good to them that love God, to them who are the called according to his purpose. Some ministers teach that this verse of scripture basically states that if you love God and you are called according to his purpose, then anything and everything you experience is necessary for you to be equipped for your purpose. A caveat to this point is that, because God is not wasteful in our experiences, he can use them, if we learn from it, as a method of helping us along the way to getting to our destiny. However, obedience to God's word or his voice could and often does eliminate this factor from occurring in the first place. There is an adage that states: the best lessons are those you pay for. In other words, experience is the best teacher. I don't believe that is what scripture teaches, but it does make for encouraging sermons on Sunday mornings.

This next point will probably anger some theologians, Bible scholars, and the like because they usually look to the sufferings of biblical characters like Job to discount or discredit such assertions. This is based on the doctrinal view that suffering is necessary for us to identify with the sufferings of Christ and to develop Christ-like character to be made fit to reign with Christ in the millennial period. Some also teach that the devil is responsible for all the bad or evil things that happen in our lives. Others teach that some things happen simply because God wills it to be and that there is nothing that can be done to avoid it or change it. This view also states that God is in control of everything in life, including your thoughts and actions, so whatever negative your experience is God's will, even if it violates his word because he is sovereign. Some of these theological views are based on different doctrinal views held by different church denominations and are used in the teaching of scripture. Other views contradict the teachings of scripture. These points are not the focus of this book, but they are being mentioned here to acknowledge that scholars, theologians, biblical historians, and pastors alike recognize a cause for bad things happening to "good people." The principle to consider in any of the cases mentioned above is that, not every decision is ordained by God, and that the law of seedtime and harvest is always at work. When this principle of seedtime and harvest is recognized as a law, then it becomes apparent why it is necessary to teach it as a law or principle to live by. Understanding this law and how it works can help you and me to be intentional in our decision making as well as in our actions so that this law works for us and not against us. This law can be used to serve humanity as God intended, or it can be ignorantly activated to work against us and all our efforts. This law is not just for agricultural purposes of producing and growing crops for human consumption, but for other purposes as well in the earth to help or improve life on the earth.

APPLYING THOUGHTS AS SEEDS

When it comes to applying your thoughts as a seed, remember the following principles:

PRINCIPLE 1. You must first identify what you are thinking about or identify your own thoughts.

HOW TO APPLY PRINCIPLE 1. Examine your own thoughts and beliefs about God, scripture, His son, etc. or anything else that relates to God. This is to help you identify where you are and any objections or internal oppositions within you. Once you identify your thoughts, go to God's word to find scriptural truth concerning what you are thinking about. Examine your own thoughts and compare them against scripture. Your thoughts must be based on truth (God's original information), not emotions, experiences, knowledge, intellect, what others have taught you, etc.

This means you must know and be aware of what you are thinking about because there is a tendency that whatever you consistently think about influences your feelings or your emotions. There is a principle in scripture which states, as a man thinks in his heart, so is he. This means you are what you think you are, or you will act based on how you think. This is important to know because your feelings follow whatever you are focused on, and concentrated thinking amplifies or magnifies whatever you are thinking about, which causes your emotions to intensify. This concentrated thinking is referred to as meditation. Meditation is a principle of rolling over repeatedly in your mind a specific thought or idea to renew your thinking or to get to the core of truth. Because of this, people will act in accordance with what they think, what they feel, or what they believe is true, right, or correct. This is true biblically, psychologically, and emotionally. If you reflect on the times in your life when you were happy, sad, angry, or scared, there is a possibility that you acted in accordance with how you were feeling. If you were in an argument, were you calm and pleasant? Were you subdued or unengaged? Were you passionately intense, or angrily expressive? Whatever the case may have been, there is a high probability that you felt some kind of way about the situation. Those emotions may have influenced you to yell and scream, throw or break things, slam doors, storm out of a room, or launch out into attack mode against others. I am using these as examples of what people may have done when they were angry. If you were happy, excited, scared, or even sexually aroused, you experienced some kind of emotions, and for too many of us, those emotions lead us to some kind of action. Once you are aware of your thoughts, you can move on to principle 2.

Principle 2. Consider if what you are thinking is helpful or harmful to you or your situation.

How to apply Principle 2. Assess the results of your way of thinking. If your thoughts are harmful to you, examine why they are harmful to you, and examine why. If you are getting the results you want, examine why. Then examine them according to scripture. Even if thoughts are helpful, it does not mean it is truth

(God's original information). Pray scripture concerning your thoughts, whether helpful or harmful. Some scripture you can use is Prov 3:5-6; Prov 16:3; Is 55:8-9. We do not naturally think the way God does, so we need Him to reveal to us His thoughts and help us to think like Him.

Being aware of your thoughts and reflecting on them requires that you are PRESENT at the moment. Being present means that you don't let your emotions run wild and get the best of you in the heat of the moment, even when you think or believe that you are right and someone else is wrong. Your thoughts and emotions are yours, not theirs, and you are responsible for what you think, what you say, and what you do. You are not responsible for what others think, say, or do. Once you recognize what your thoughts are, move on to principle 3.

Principle 3. Align your thinking with scriptural standards.

How to apply Principle 3. Decide that God's word will be your standard for how

you think and the decisions you will make.

Part of changing your thoughts means learning that God thinks differently and learning how he thinks, then adapt to his way of thinking. This will help you change your thoughts through prayer and applying His word.

You are probably saying to yourself, that's easier said than done! I agree with you; it's not easy to change your thoughts when you are in the middle of a heated exchange or if you are feeling emotional in a situation. Change in any situation is rarely easy, but in most situations is necessary. You and I must be spiritually and emotionally mature and disciplined enough to stop ourselves from going over an emotional cliff whenever someone else pushes our emotional buttons. This point here will test your spiritual and emotional resolve because if you believe you are justified in your feelings and someone else has crossed the line with you, disrespected you, or offended you, you may want to give them a piece of your mind, defend yourself, or protect yourself. However, if you find yourself repeating behavioral patterns that are not helpful to you, then at some point you must decide that you want the madness to end, and do something different, and this requires you to change. There is an adage that states insanity is doing the same thing repeatedly but expecting different results. Many people do things that are damaging and destructive to themselves but never change their thinking or their actions, and as a result, nothing else in their lives changes either. This is important to know because the good news is that if you want to change your life, you need to change your thoughts. When you change your thoughts, you can change your feelings, your words, what you are listening to, and change what you are watching. In other words, you can change your focus. Several scriptures provide alternative ways of thinking. For example, one scripture says you and I must cast down imaginations and every high thing that exalts itself against the knowledge of God and brings every thought captive to the obedience of Christ. This means you can exchange what you think by replacing that thought with a biblical thought that is to your advantage. Another scripture says God will keep you in perfect peace if your mind remains fixed on him. In other words, focusing on God, his word, his promises, his might, his abilities, and all of his other attributes will bring peace of mind because your focus is on him and not your circumstances. There is another one that says, keep your mind on whatever is true, pure, right, holy, friendly, and proper. Don't ever stop thinking about what is truly worthwhile and worthy of praise. Romans 10:17 states that faith comes by hearing and hearing by the word of God. In other words, what you are hearing affects what you believe is true, and as a result, affects your thoughts and actions in life. Once you change your thoughts, move on to principle 4.

PRINCIPLE 4. Begin immersing yourself in the scriptures.

HOW TO APPLY PRINCIPLE 4. By immersing your ears, eyes, heart, and your mouth with information from Gods' word, you will begin to transfer God's thoughts to you and transform what you think, feel, believe, or speak about your life and your circumstances. This also causes you to change your perspective or how you see the situation as well as your response.

The more of God's word you input in your heart, the more of his thoughts, ideas, images, and solutions begin to replace the old thoughts and ideas in your mind. The scripture states that we have the mind of Christ. This becomes true when you put the word of God in your heart and meditate on it. It is vital to implement these principles and immerse yourself in God's word to renew your mind and thinking.

AUGUST 9, 2014

Now imagine if someone used words or images to tell stories painting pictures in the mind of others, causing them to have an emotional or visceral reaction based upon the words or stories they heard. How powerful would that be? What kind of power or influence that would be?

We have seen these kinds of powerful images, words, and influences at different times in modern history. We saw it, heard it, and felt it when Dr. Martin Luther King Jr. gave his famous "I Have a

Dream" speech in front of the Lincoln Memorial in Washington D.C in August of 1963 (The King Center, 2019). Many believed at that time there was hope for the nation to end racial segregation, riots, and protests, and that equal opportunities and fair treatment for all Americans were possible and could be achieved if people were treated not based on the color of their skin but by the content of their character. We saw it, heard it, and we felt it with the fall of the Berlin Wall in November of 1989, ending the Cold War. The fall symbolized the pathway to freedom for those oppressed between East Berlin and West Berlin. We experienced it with the attacks on and the collapse of the World Trade Center Twin Towers in Manhattan, New York September 11, 2001 (History.com, 2018). We saw how a handful of determined radical Muslim extremists introduced fear into the American psyche using terrorism and fear as their weapons of mass destruction. We also experienced it in my hometown on August 9, 2014 (Suggs, 2014). Images of eighteen-year-old Michael Brown lying dead in the middle of the street of the Canfield Apartments after being killed by Ferguson police officer Darren Wilson flooded every television station around the country. The images of his dead body lying in the street for four hours and the outrage expressed in the form of rioting by the people of that community reverberated around the world.

Repeated images of anarchy, looting, people destroying property, and clashes with the police created angst, terror, and uncertainty for the people of Ferguson, Missouri, and for some across the country in other urban centers. People who had experienced any perceived incidences of racial injustice at the hands of law enforcement were bitter and felt that another unarmed black man had been executed by police with impunity. Many believed that their children were no longer safe and could longer expect to leave home, encounter the police, and return home safe or alive. These were some of the sentiments being expressed by the public on local and national media outlets, in town hall meetings, in barbershops, salons, in churches as well as by activists, political commentators, and national civil rights leaders. These fears reignited the conversation surrounding Second Amendment rights, stand your ground laws, the rights of business owners to preserve and protect property, along with discussion surrounding civil rights and personal safety.

The images of protesters and rioters clashing with law enforcement and the National Guard in Ferguson, Missouri only showed the actions of a relatively small number of people along a five-block strip of West Florissant Boulevard, yet these images gave the impression that all of St. Louis was up in arms. If you were not from St. Louis, involved in law enforcement, or have never had experience in urban warfare or crowd control, then you would have been under the impression that the entire St. Louis area was under Marshall Law. Many of those participants did not actually live in St. Louis, nor were they from the area, but were actually paid protestors from other states (Chowdhury, 2014). Nevertheless, those images and the fears created from these encounters led to a drastic rise in the sale of handguns, semi-automatic weapons, and ammunition purchases (" Gun Sales Spike Around Ferguson After 3 Days of Riots", 2015). People began enrolling in firearms training, obtaining firearms permits, and taking self-defense classes (Crilly, Allen, Khan, & Alexander, 2014). These feelings and sentiments also gave greater national exposure to the Black Lives Matter movement and other grassroots organizations creating a resurgence in social activism among urban millennials (Friedersdorf, 2015). It also gave increased national attention to the growing Alt-right movement, which focuses on white nationalism, reverse discrimination, and a return to a Jim Crow-era America (Gray, 2019). This single event lit the spark that spread like wildfire across the country, rehashing biases that have existed for decades along the lines of race and economics in America. These narratives and images were influencing the emotions of many

Americans and were shaping the perspective and belief systems of multitudes, creating an atmosphere of division along the lines of race and class. The idea I want to drill home to you is that a picture (thought/idea) is worth a thousand words. Those thoughts/images were affecting what people thought, felt, believed, and how they behaved.

These same tactics are used by media, marketers, advertisers, and PR firms to affect the bottom line of for-profit corporations. They use poignant images that will prick the emotions of potential customers by displaying private, tender moments of innocence and vulnerability or the worst of human behavior, set to replay hundreds of times to create a reaction, an emotion, a memory and a call to action to purchase their goods, products or services. If this is what can be done to influence the masses to produce a profit for corporations by getting them to purchase a product, going to the movies, or voting for a political candidate, then imagine what other possible ways people can be influenced or manipulated in their thinking and emotions. Well, that is exactly what happens daily when people watch the news, watch a movie, listen to music or listen to speeches, presentations, and debates. People become influenced by the words and storytelling of marketers and advertisers every day, and that influence translates into business profits because ideas and messages are being disbursed to the masses in seed form. Every message is the seed that influences others to act. Before anyone has resolved their belief system in their own heart, they usually go through a process to determine what ideas they value and possess, and the origin of those ideas. Those ideas establish the foundation for their philosophy or worldview. This worldview establishes what a person believes, why they think the way they think, how they see themselves, what they believe they have to contribute to the world, and how they will live in the world. These are all examples of thoughts as seeds producing a harvest in the lives of others.

You must be intentional with what you feed yourself in terms of information, news, or other content that builds and reinforces what you accept as being true. You must also focus your attention on it through meditation. When you meditate, you are rolling thoughts over in your mind, muttering with your mouth repeatedly to engrave upon your heart what you want to be produced out of your heart. This process will work with anything you want your heart to produce. It is in your best interest to make sure you are meditating on God's word so that you can begin to produce the promises of God in your own life, but you must get into his word to know it for yourself. You must know what he wants to be accomplished by you and through you, and you must be laser-focused on that mission. You cannot allow yourself to be deceived, discouraged, or distracted by what you see being promoted by faith killing media outlets. You must decide that I will see the goodness of the lord in the land of the living. You must decide and make a plan of action about how you can make God's will be known or make him well known in a generation that seems to not have any interest in God? You must take your plan to him and get his heart, his mind, his will, and allow Him to direct your path. Then and only then will your plans succeed. Proverbs 3:5-6 says: Trust in the Lord with all thine heart and lean not to thy own understanding; in all thy ways acknowledge him, and he shall direct thy path. Proverbs 16:3 says it this way: Commit thy works unto the Lord, and thy thoughts shall be established.

6
WORDS AS A SEED

Genesis chapter one and John chapter one both communicate the next principle we will discuss, and that is the principle of words as seeds. Genesis states, in the beginning, God created the heavens and the earth. It states God said something, and what he said came to pass and was manifested. The book of John says that God's word was in the beginning, and that God and his word were one. The Genesis account also provides a record and an explanation for the creation of all that exists and is known to man based solely on the words spoken by God. In other words, everything that God created, he created with his words. The scripture also teaches a principle which most belief systems around the world accept as undeniable truth; the principle is this: Life and Death are in the power of the tongue. This principle is communicating the idea that life or death is affected by your tongue or, more specifically, your words. This idea means that you and I have the same ability as God to create, shape, and influence our world based on the words we speak. This is a spiritual principle or law that is taught in most belief systems and works no matter who you are. This principle, according to scripture, says it another way. In the book of Mark 11:23 it states, whosoever shall say to the mountain (the problem), be thou removed and be thou cast into the sea, and shall not doubt in his heart but shall believe the things he says shall come to pass, he shall have whatsoever he says. This scripture is highlighting a specific point. It did not say that if you say something, what you say will come to pass, it says if you believe in your heart the words you speak will come to pass, then you will have what you say.

Another reason why this is important to understand is the fact that, in scripture, God always keeps his word. Man was made in the image and likeness of God and is expected by God to also keep his words, and when we say something, it is expected for us to keep our words. This is so important to understand because God keeps (performs) his word even when we don't. It is also recorded in scripture that God holds man accountable for our words to him. The scripture refers to this as making a vow to God. Whenever someone made a promise, a pledge, or a vow to God and did not keep it, this act was considered being separated from our word, or lying, and would cost a man his life. The scriptures give this admonition: it is better to not vow a vow to the Lord than to vow and not keep it. Why should you let your flesh cause you to sin? In other words, you and I must say what we mean, mean what we say, keep our word, and we must believe our own words. When you believe your words have the power to manifest what you say, you begin to choose your words carefully and be more intentional and specific with what you say and how you say it. What I am describing is not black magic, voodoo, incantations, spells, curses, or witchcraft, but it is a spiritual law and widely practiced in most religions.

Another element in law is that our words and intentions, when spoken, affect physical matter because of the vibrations of our words and voice. This ought not to be something viewed as spooky or superstitious because, in truth, we are imitating God when he created the heavens and the earth according to the scriptures recorded in Genesis 1:1-31. Our words carry the substance of intentions, and when they are spoken with power, with passion and intention, we manifest what we say. It does not occur overnight, but over time and it will eventually manifest because it was spoken from the heart or from the core of our being. Many times, we will speak the desires of our hearts repeatedly, which programs our hearts to believe our words, and eventually, our words will bring about a physical manifestation. This principle works both positively and negatively. In the U.S. during the 1990s and early 2000s, there was a laundry list artists and musicians who recorded albums and CD's with questionable lyrics that spoke of them dying early in life, and for some within a few years and others a few days, the very words they spoke on their albums came to pass. People referred to this as being prophetic, but in truth, these artists and musicians were operating a principle or law that states death and life are in the power of the tongue. I want to encourage you to take inventory of the words you have been speaking about yourself, your marriage, your children, your job or business, your health, your finances, or any other area of your life. Evaluate whether or not if you have been speaking life to your situation and circumstances or have you been speaking death. You may say to yourself, "I don't believe that my words will affect my situation." That may be true if you don't believe your own words when you speak positively, but what about when you speak negatively? Are you absolutely convinced that only bad and negative things happen or will happen to you? Do you have a negative expectation for bad things happening to you? Maybe it is partly because you expect it and secondly because you keep speaking it. You have to decide to start speaking what you want to happen in your life instead of agreeing with your negative past and expecting to experience more of the same.

We often see the results of our words coming to pass when we see the laws of the land change because we desire change, or the change of public policies because we want policies to change. Sometimes we make calls for justice, we demand revenge for injustice, or simply speak affirmations for our financial and career success or for our hopes, dreams, and desires. It is passion, the fear, our expectations, and the intentions behind our words that make them come to pass because our words are the containers of our intentions. There is an adage that states: sticks and stones may break my bones, but words will never harm me. This statement is not always true. Words might not physically hurt a person, but they can definitely wound, cut, and damage our emotions and affect our sense of self-esteem, self-image, and identity. This happens many times because the words spoken were intended to injury the recipient of the message. Many times, young people have attempted suicide because of the hurtful and hateful rhetoric mean and spiteful people have spoken to them or about them. Sensitive people often respond with offense that is turned inward to abuse themselves or lash out at others with equally destructive behavior, as seen on local news. There have been countless news stories around the country that report random acts of violence or mass shootings committed by people who felt rejected, insulted, offended, or bullied by the words of others. Our words have the potential of influencing the thoughts, ideas, and opinions of others because not only do they affect their emotions, but they also influence their mental state and their behavior. Our words can paint images and pictures in the mind of people that is nothing more than an opinion, but a person can internalize it and believe it is the truth. It is not being suggested that you or I are responsible for the decisions of others, but we all have a responsibility for how we speak to and treat others. Part of that responsibility involves how we use our words. Are we using our words to inspire, encourage, give hope, express possibilities of success, or are we using our words as tools to deceive, distract, discourage, or destroy the hope, faith, and expectations of others?

Whenever you decide you want to say something, keep the following principles in mind.

APPLYING WORDS AS SEEDS

Principle 1. Words have the power of life or death.

HOW TO APPLY PRINCIPLE 1. You must get control of your tongue and train your mouth on how to speak correctly.

This is one of the most powerful points you will ever learn because your words have the power of life and death. The words you speak can affect you and others. You hear yourself speak more than any other person, and your voice is the most influential in your life. What others say to you or about you is not as important as what you say to yourself or about yourself. The words you speak come out of your own heart, so the words you speak to yourself or about yourself also affects what you think, feel, or believe about yourself. Too often people will say that they are keeping it real, or calling things as they see it. The problem with this mindset is that keeping it real often translates to keeping it negative. Calling it as you see it often translates to walking by sight and not living by faith. Some may say that they would be lying if they said anything other than what they see. Honestly, it is easier and more natural to speak what you see, especially if you don't have a spiritual point of reference. Without the understanding of spiritual reality, your perspective will always be limited because all you know is based on what you see. There is so much more than what you and I can see with our eyes or perceive with our five physical senses. If you are unaware of the endless resources, possibilities, and answers that God has to fix your situation, then your view on life will be bleak and pessimistic. However, when you realize that God cannot say "I don't know" because he is all-knowing, then you can begin to take comfort and rest in the truth that God has my answer and based on this truth, I can speak life to my situation and not death to change it.

Principle 2. Words express your thinking and emotional state

How to Apply Principle 2. You must get control of your emotions and not allow yourself to speak based solely on your emotional state.

This can be very difficult for a multitude of reasons, but it is not impossible. Since we all have emotions, we often speak from the place of how we feel. Some of us are more emotional or sensitive than others, which makes controlling our emotions that much more challenging. This can be intensified if our upbringing was such that we had to fight to be seen or heard or if we were raised to not have a filter on our communication. To not speak would be the equivalent of censorship, and in the U.S. the freedom of speech is not only a constitutionally protected right by law, but also a way of life. Many will fight you for the right to be heard, especially if they feel or believe they have been suppressed in their freedom to express their thoughts, ideas, and opinions no matter how extreme or outlandish they may be. Their focus then is to be heard, not realizing that it might not be in their own best interest in giving everyone a piece of their mind or always saying how you feel. We all have emotions and have a right to feel however we may feel, but spiritually, speaking based on your feelings set things in motion in your life that can come back to you or backfire on you. We should all take the time to think before we speak or as scripture admonishes, be quick to hear, slow to speak, and slow to wrath.

Principle 3. You will only have what you say, not what others say.

How to Apply Principle 3. Decide what you want in life and only speak in line with that expectation.

Many distractions in the world fight and compete for our attention daily, and they can be both positive or negative. Sometimes if something good or bad happens to us or someone close to us, there can be a temptation to imagine the same things happening to us. It is in these moments that we must decide what do we want out of life and what kind of life we want to live. We must resist the urge to say everything that comes to our mind, especially if it is negative because in speaking it, we give the thing permission to come to us or be acceptable in our own lives. This does not mean you want it to happen to you, but it does mean that by saying that it could happen to you, you are giving room and permission for the thing to occur in your life. I know some people will disagree with this and say that this is not a realistic view of life, but life happens, and there are some things in life you cannot control. This is true; life does happen, and bad things can happen to good people, and at the same time, you can control what you say to yourself, about yourself, and about your circumstances and situations. You have complete control over what you say, that is your choice.

Principle 4. God confirms his word with signs following, so speak His word.

. . .

HOW TO APPLY PRINCIPLE 4. You must train your mouth to speak the promises of God in every situation.

If you accept God's words as truth, and you expect him to perform his word, then you will always have confidence in his promises when you speak them. You will develop the habit of saying what God says, knowing that what he says will not be empty words. When you say what God said in his word, you are making a confession. A confession is saying what God says. Another way of making a confession is to speak the truth. God's word is truth, and when you speak His word about a situation, you are making a confession. This becomes a way of life for those who experience the promises of God manifested in their own lives. They begin to no longer be moved emotionally by the events occurring around them because they have accumulated experiences that validate and confirm for them that God and his word can be trusted. Let me also say this for the intellectual; everything that has just been stated is subjective for the person who accepts it as being true. The scripture says it this way, all things are possible to him that believes, and with God, nothing shall be impossible, so speak the promises of God into your circumstances and watch what others call impossible become possible for you.

7
SOWING VERSUS GIVING PRINCIPLE

Let me also explain another spiritual aspect of seedtime and harvest called sowing. This addresses the distinction between the principle of sowing versus the principle of giving. Giving is an activity people engage in when they are attempting to help those in need, such as individuals or families who may be experiencing a temporary economic setback. Sometimes people give or provide resources to organizations that serve large segments of the population that are chronically in need. Because of this scenario, some people who have the means to give, choose not to, or may not have the motivation or incentive to give because of a perception of poor people manipulating or abusing social service programs, charities, non-profit organizations, or the good-hearted nature of those who want to help people in need. They may believe it is better to help those in a third world nation instead of those on the other side of town. Unfortunately, it also prevents others who may genuinely need receiving life-sustaining assistance because of these perceptions. Whenever you give, however, you are demonstrating faith toward God and love toward others. God says whatever you do to the least of these, you have done it to me. Giving is sometimes referred to as charity, such as giving to the poor and needy. Sometimes the act of giving demonstrates compassion on others in need, but sometimes it doesn't.

In fact, I recently heard a different perspective on the subject that shocked me, and because of how brash the comment was, I initially would have never considered the idea until he mentioned it. The idea is that the reason why some people give to the poor is to simply make them go away. What? In other words, the idea goes like this: if I give you some change, will you just go away and leave me alone? The statement was blunt, brash, but honest for some people. The statement was made by a wealthy, type-A personality businessman and the context of the statement centered around giving to homeless people on highway ramps and street intersections. He stated that if a homeless person asks you if you could "help" them and you give them a nickel, a dime, or a quarter, you didn't really "help" them; you simply gave them some change to make them go away. He further stated that if you really wanted to help them, you should give them something that could make a difference in their lives, like maybe a thousand dollars or more. Maybe you could give them a job or connect them to some other opportunity that would really help them and change their circumstances. The businessman concluded his commentary by stating that those who respond to homeless people or others in need in this manner truly believe they are being generous, are helping people, and feel good about themselves. If there are others who knowingly or unknowingly think this way, it cannot be overstated that these folks are not being generous, nor are they demonstrating the love of God. Yes, the person did give, but that is not the only idea behind giving. Giving to others is an expression of love to the recipient of the gift, and it is also an extension of oneself to others.

Sowing, however, is different. Sowing is God-directed giving/releasing. Sowing is activated when you hear and obey the voice of God or the spirit of God to release something specific to a specific person or to others that he instructs you. It is the specific instruction of the Lord to you that makes sowing unique. Sometimes, God may instruct you to sow (release) something to someone that you don't know, or not even like. Sowing has nothing to do with your preference toward someone. However, it has everything to do with obedience toward God. Sowing is much different from just giving and showing love and compassion for others. When you give to others, hopefully, you are helping them, but when you sow, you are obeying God's voice or God's instructions to you personally and accomplishing the will of God in some capacity. Sowing is a law that works whether you agree with the instruction or not, and your act of obedience to sow puts you in a better position to receive what some call a "supernatural return" on your seed sown. This is the difference between doing a good thing and doing a God-directed thing. When you give to others, you are obeying the written word of God (Prov. 19:17). When you sow to others, you are obeying the voice of God, which is an instruction to you and for you. The instruction you receive is referred to as a "rhema word," which simply means a now, in the moment, instruction from God himself. This distinction is the difference between those who live an average life and those who live a supernatural life.

In the Bible, if you read Luke chapter 5, you will see an account where Jesus asks a fisherman named Simon (Peter) to use his fishing boat as a platform to teach to a crowd of people who came to hear him speak. Simon allows Jesus to get into his boat and use it to teach the multitudes. When Jesus finishes, he gives Simon an instruction to launch out into the deep and let down his nets for a draught (a huge catch of fish). Peter obeys the instructions given by Jesus, although he doesn't believe anything will happen. He also tells Jesus that he and his fishing partners have been fishing all night and haven't caught any fish, but nevertheless, at Jesus' word, he would do it. What is unique in this story are two distinct points. The first point is that Simon allowed his boat to be used by

Jesus for "ministry" purposes. Simon was not using it at the time, he did not catch any fish, and he did not ask Jesus for money to rent his boat, so in a sense, he donated his boat for Jesus' mission. The second point is that Jesus now gives instruction to Simon, and he simply follows the instruction because he respects Jesus, not because he believes anything will happen. Obedience to Jesus' instruction, however, caused Peter to experience the greatest catch of fish in his entire career as a fisherman. Peter's obedience not only affected Peter, but also impacted his fishing business, and his business partners. Not only did Peter prosper from one act of obedience, but so did his partners. Peter was the only one who heard the instruction and obeyed the instruction, yet others were affected by his obedience. The same thing could or might have happened to you when you simply obeyed an instruction from God.

When you talk to those who obeyed the voice of God, they usually have a testimony, a story, or an experience of unusual and supernatural events occurring in their lives. Many others have obeyed an instruction from God have had things happen to them that cannot be explained logically, in terms of how they happened, except to say that God blessed them because they obeyed his voice.

In my own life, one act of obedience to an instruction from God led to a two-year season of unexplained blessings. Things happened to my wife and me materially, financially, and in other areas of our lives that we didn't have the natural ability to make happen. When we examined our lives, and the only thing we could conclude to explain how things happened was that we simply obeyed God, and He blessed our obedience. Family members and friends who had firsthand knowledge of our financial circumstances were scratching their heads, trying to figure out how these things were happening to us. The only thing they knew was that our situation looked one way for a few years, and then we acted in obedience to an instruction from God, and suddenly things were instantly different for us.

We didn't become multimillionaires or anything like that, but there were some very specific things occurring in our lives that could not be explained logically. We weren't making all the right decisions in our lives at the time, and we didn't live perfect or flawless lives, but what was crystal clear was that one act of obedience to God and his word changed our lives. The impact was so great that others wanted to start learning about God, the Bible, come to church, and get to know God for themselves. This is what obedience to God can do; it will affect those around you or those who are watching you and draw them closer to God. This was the first time I began to understand why a person being blessed by God was not about them, but about God wanting to demonstrate his goodness in someone's life. I saw how he wanted to put people on display who he chose to bless to bring attention to himself and draw others to himself. I began to see how God honors his word in the lives of those that choose to trust, honor, and obey him. This is the one common denominator I have found that consistently happens for people who obey an instruction from God. When this happens, it defies logic, reason, and natural law because one act or seed of obedience to an instruction from God accelerates a persons' life, a family, a business, a ministry, an industry, or a nation into a season of blessing, which some call success, but only God can take the credit for it.

From a logical and financial perspective, sowing is similar to investing. It is similar to investing in the sense that, when you sow a seed or act of obedience, it is almost guaranteed that what you receive back (ROI) will be much greater than what you sowed (invested). The reason people become investors in the first place is that they want their money to work hard for them instead of them working hard for their money. When someone invests their money, resources, or capital, they are expecting a return on their investment that accomplishes more than what the investor could accomplish using their own physical abilities. When you give in response to an instruction from God, the harvest behind your obedience will produce results that you cannot take credit for; only God can get the credit, and you will be the better for it. Let me be clear, sowing is not natural investing even though there are some striking similarities, but sowing is investing in the kingdom of God and will always produce better results than what natural investing can produce. Sowing produces kingdom results because sowing is acting in obedience, and obedience is an act of advancing God's kingdom.

APPLYING THE PRINCIPLE OF GIVING

When it comes to applying the principle of giving, remember and apply the following principles.

PRINCIPLE 1. Giving is a Law, and everyone can be a Giver.

HOW TO APPLY PRINCIPLE 1. Give what you have that can be useful and helpful to others. Avoid giving something to others that you would not want someone to give to you, unless God instructs otherwise. Giving is a law like gravity, which affects everyone who turns it on. When you know that what you give comes back to you in greater measure, you are more likely to give and doing it frequently. The effect can be what some call "paying it forward," or a chain reaction of people giving to others because someone else gave to them.

PRINCIPLE 2. Decide that you will be a generous giver.

. . .

HOW TO APPLY PRINCIPLE 2. Give to others in the manner and at the level you would want others to give to you. The principle here is to do unto others as you would have them do unto you. This does not mean that you give indiscriminately to others or with reckless abandonment to your own demise. It does mean, however, that when you do it, you want them to know that what you gave came from God through your hands, and in return, God will bless your socks off. Lastly, remember that giving always requires making a decision first that you will give to others when you have the opportunity.

PRINCIPLE 3. Be intentional about what you give and how you give.

HOW TO APPLY PRINCIPLE 3. Decide what you will give and how you will do it. This means that, not only are you making the decision to give to others, but you are being discriminate about who you give to, and what you give them. Giving does not always involve giving money. Sometimes your giving might involve donating your time as a volunteer, being a mentor to someone, or serving others with your gifts, talents, or skills. Sometimes it might be best to give counsel or sound advice to someone in need of direction or who may need help in making a quality decision.

PRINCIPLE 4. Never allow your giving to be conditional or with strings attached.

HOW TO APPLY PRINCIPLE 4. Do not give to others expecting them to do something for you in return. That is called bribery and manipulation. If you are expecting the person to repay you, then all you did was give them a loan. If you expect some kind of "quid pro quo" or this for that, then you demonstrate you want them to do you a favor, and God has no part in what you are doing.

Remember this point: treat others the way you would treat God. I know that is hard for some to comprehend, but when you realize that the way you treat others demonstrates how you would treat God, it will completely change how you view and respond to them. Your giving should never be used to manipulate others. That kind of giving makes interactions conditional; it puts a strain on relationships; it makes people suspicious about your motives and causes them to question if you have a real relationship with them or not.

PRINCIPLE 5. Giving is a heart issue.

HOW TO APPLY PRINCIPLE 5. Give because you choose to give, not because you have to or because you feel compelled or manipulated to give. Be sincere with your gift-giving. If a picture is worth a thousand words, then a gift is worth a thousand gestures. Your gift can sometimes express things in ways that sometimes your words fall short.

What this means is that giving demonstrates your desire to connect with others. When you are a giver, you get joy from seeing the lives of others being touched by your gift(s). What is also clear is that, if it is not in your heart to give to others, then you won't give.

PRINCIPLE 6. Giving demonstrates the heart of God.

HOW TO APPLY PRINCIPLE 6. Give whenever you have the opportunity. Give to help others. Give to meet a need. Give to create opportunities for others. Give generously. Give to inspire others to be generous. Give to overcome greed. Give anonymously.

Become God's distribution center of giving. Scripture reveals that the nature of God is to give and what better way for us to demonstrate that nature than to give to others. Scripture teaches that God is Love, but love is demonstrated in four ways: giving, investing of time with others, serving others, and sacrificing for others. Scripture teaches that God gave man life, breath, and all things. It also states that God loved the world so much that he gave his only begotten son.'

APPLYING THE PRINCIPLE OF SOWING

When it comes to applying the principle of sowing, it is necessary to keep the following principles in mind.

PRINCIPLE 1. Sowing is God-directed giving.

HOW TO APPLY PRINCIPLE 1. Because it is God-directed, only sow when God instructs, directs, or inspires you to sow. Never sow if God has not instructed, directed, or led you to sow; that is called giving.

As stated previously, sowing or God-directed giving means just that; God is directing your giving. You are not sowing because you want to do a good deed, or because you want to be recognized for charity, or you want to help someone in need, or you want to get a large return on your giving. When you sow your seed, you are submitting yourself to an instruction from God for something he wants to do for someone else. Again, I want to remind you that sowing is an act of obedience to Gods' instruction and does not always involve giving money or something of monetary value, but there is always an action or transaction on your part of obedience to God.

Principle 2. Sowing is an act of obedience.

How to apply Principle 2. Be quick to obey God in your sowing with whatever he instructs.

He will not tell you to do something you cannot do or give you something you do not have, so don't complicate things with foolish questions about "what if he tells me to give a million dollars that I don't have?" He won't give that kind of instruction unless he knows that you have it and are willing to give it. When you sow, you are choosing to obey God with whatever it is that you have, that God wants to bless others with, through your act of obedience. When you obey God with your giving, you are also demonstrating your desire to please him and not pleasing or impressing others.

Principle 3. Sowing is not an emotional event.

How to apply Principle 3. Sowing requires being intentional and taking action and is not about how you feel or don't feel about the situation.

This point is very important because sometimes you might get an instruction to sow to someone you don't like or may not agree with. Let me say something to you regarding this point. God is interested in his purpose and his will being accomplished. It is for this reason that you must understand that he is more interested in his will than your feelings. Your feelings can sometimes stand in the way of your next season of extraordinary living that gets hindered because you are in your feelings, offended, put off, or whatever excuse you choose to use. This comes from a sense of pride, self-righteousness, and a false sense of entitlement to hold on to the idea of not being wrong, disrespected, or mistreated. I'm not suggesting that you allow people to mistreat you, but I am saying that if God instructs you to bless someone by sowing into their lives, your obedience or rebellion will determine what will or won't happen in your life and that of others, Sometimes you might get an instruction to give to causes that you have no interest in at all. When that is the case, you cannot allow your feelings or emotions to interfere with your obedience.

PRINCIPLE 4. Obey completely.

HOW TO APPLY PRINCIPLE 4. Only do what God instructs, nothing more, nothing less.

There is an account in scripture in the book of 1 Samuel 15 involving King Saul. God instructed him through the prophet Samuel to destroy the Amalekites, the enemies of God's people, Israel. The king partially obeyed and preserved the life of King Agag along with the best animals King Agag had. When King Saul is confronted about his partial obedience, he states that he feared the people. This partial obedience (disobedience) caused him to lose his kingdom, his life, and the life of one of his sons. Don't do what you think God said to do, do what he said to do and don't add anything to it. In other words, obey the instructions completely when you sow your seed and don't add to his instructions or take away from them. If God instructs you to give $1,000, give the full amount and not $10 or $100. If he instructs you to buy groceries for someone, pay a bill for someone, or take them shopping for new clothes, just do it. If he tells you to give a family the car you are not using, give it to them. Don't just offer them a ride somewhere occasionally. If he instructs you to invite someone to live in your home rent-free, do it. Don't give something or do something God didn't ask you to do. If you do this, your giving will not be blessed by God, and you will be doing something God didn't say do, and you will have a bad attitude about doing it. Don't ignore the instructions, either. When you ignore him, you sow a seed of disobedience that becomes a harvest of being ignored or neglected by God when you need him. You may say, I don't believe that because God loves everyone and provides for everyone. You are correct! He does love everyone, and he does provide for everyone, through those that choose to obey him when he instructs them to sow their seed. If you don't believe this, you should read what the scripture says in Galatians 6:7, Be not deceived, for God is not mocked, whatever a man sows, that is what he also reaps. It also states in Luke 6:38, Give, and it shall be given unto you; good measure, pressed down, shaken together and running over, shall men give unto your bosom. For with the same measure you mete withal it shall be measured to you again. Let me say one final thing also about sowing. Everything that has been shared so far about sowing presumes that you are someone who has a relationship with God, and you pray to God, you recognize God's voice, you read God's word, you study God's word, you have a desire to please God, your heart is open to God, and you desire to be used by God. If this does not describe you, sowing will be something that will be difficult for you to do. You won't do it because you will be judging, evaluating, and assessing the situation based on your own intellect apart from God, apart from his word, and apart from the leading of his spirit, plus you won't have the capacity to judge righteous judgment because you don't understand how God operates through his people.

8

DAY AND NIGHT (THE CYCLE PRINCIPLE)

The next principle mentioned in Genesis 8:22 is that day and night shall not cease. The phrase shall not cease is the Hebrew word for Sabbath or Shabath. Sabbath is the seventh day of the week, and the only day where God establishes it as a day of rest for humanity. Every seven days, there is at least one day, God commands everyone to rest from all their labor except for worship to God. To rest means to cease from all labor, all work, and all action. What this means, however, is that although there is a day of rest or a Sabbath, rest does not apply to the existence of day and night.

Therefore, God says there is no rest for the evening and the morning; it is a cycle, a pattern, a revolution of time, and an activity that repeats every twenty-four hours. This cycle also establishes the parameters for our modern-day time clock cycle of twenty-four hours. Life is measured by time and experiences. Time is also measured by clocks, calendars, timetables, seasons, and schedules based on the cycle of day and night, not ceasing. It means there is no end to the cycle of night and day on planet earth. There will always be nighttime and a daytime while the earth remains. This cycle has no expiration date. This principle or law of time began in Genesis 1:5. It tells us: *"And God called the light Day, and the darkness he called Night. And the evening and the morning were the first day."* Again, this evening and morning established a cycle, which means *a complete series or round of occurrences that repeats or is repeated.* It is also *a round of years or a recurring period of time, especially when certain events or phenomena repeat themselves in the same order or at the same intervals.* In other words, a cycle is a series of events or a pattern of behavior that repeats itself. The cycle principle is important because many of life's events occur in cycles.

The full twenty-four-hour period of a day is a cycle. A one-week period is a cycle. A thirty-day period is a cycle. Women each month experience something that is referred to as a menstrual cycle. The reason why cycles are important to know and recognize is, cycles indicate repeating patterns. When events repeat themselves, there is the possibility of a cycle at work. When people get paid on their jobs, it is usually at the end of a two-week work period or work cycle. When politicians come up for re-election for a political office, it is referred to as an election cycle. When news is reported at five, six, and ten, it is called a news cycle. When tornados or hurricanes come through an area, it is called hurricane season (cycle) or tornado season (cycle). These are events that occur in a certain predictable pattern, which is a good thing. When you can predict when a thing will occur, it means you have identified the cycle or pattern, and now you can act accordingly to the cues when cycles begin or when they end.

This is exactly what is done in the financial arena. Individuals known as "Options Traders," "Day Traders," or "Forex Traders" utilize a concept that identifies "trends" in the market. In other words, these traders can predict which way the financial market is moving or "trending, and based on the cues whether it is trending upward, downward, or sideways, and they know what strategy they will use to invest, buy, trade, or sell to make money. These trends or cycles allow traders to trade currency pairs or stock options to maximize their profits off their trades. These traders don't care which way the market moves, because they know how to capitalize off the market and realize profits regardless of the direction of the market. They decide how much they want to make on each trade because they have developed their skill-sets, studied the market, understand the trends, know the cues and when to make their trades, and they know who the participants are, how they think and how they will move in and out of trades. All these factors make investing or trading less risky for some, while the novices gamble trying to do what the professional traders do. Without sufficient skills, knowledge of the cycles, or training, these wanna-be traders end up losing fortunes because they are guessing or speculating. Recognition of cycles, when they occur and how they happen, could have a life-changing effect for those who understand the cues for when cycles begin and end. This is just one example of the importance of understanding what cycles are, how they work, and how to use this knowledge and leverage it to your advantage (Investopedia, 2019).

THE SEVEN-YEAR CYCLE

Another example of a cycle would be what is called "The Shemitah." According to Rabbi Jonathan Cahn, author of the books, "The Harbinger" and "The Mystery of the Shemitah," every seven years is a "shemitah" or a sabbath year, aka a sabbatical year, a release from and a cancellation of debts, a financial crash, or the end of an economic cycle (Cahn, 2014). It comes from the seven-year agricultural cycle mandated in the Torah for the land of Israel for over 3000 years, which is still practiced to this day in contemporary Judaism (Sales, 2014). This has been observed and found to be accurate according to Jewish rabbis for over three millenniums and is believed to have some connection to the world financial markets.

In fact, financial analysts have discovered that major market crashes have occurred every seven years, which have been tied to world events.

According to U.S. Government Statistics, from 1966 until 2008, there have been seven major economic declines in the U.S. economy, which affected other world markets that recur in the same round of cycles with nearly the exact same pattern (Brufaldi, 2019). Part of the pattern observed is the ebb and flow of the economic cycle, which includes the Peaks, Recessions, Troughs, and Recoveries. This up and down pattern of activity establishes a cycle that can be recognized, charted, and is often used by investors to determine what financial markets will do and how best to plan for them to realize economic gains. With these kinds of patterns and tools, individual investors, private companies, governments, and financial institutions don't have to speculate on what to do with their money. They know exactly what to do, they understand the cycles and know how to capitalize on these opportunities while others who are ignorant of what's happening simply guess and pray for the best.

All of this is part of the Shemitah represents a seven-year cycle. When I initially began writing this book, the U.S. was in the early stage of the economic crisis, which began in 2007, manifested in 2008, and concluded in 2009. Since that time, much has changed. It was during that economic and political period that Barack Obama made his first bid to run for and win the U.S. presidency in 2008. His campaign slogan was Change: Yes We Can. 2008 was the end of a seven-year cycle that started in 2001 following 911 and the collapse of the World Trade Center towers. Another interesting idea that relates to seven-year cycles is the human body's biological ability to shed and replace most human cells. It is believed that the cells of all the major and minor organs of the body are replaced every seven years, which may explain why maturity and aging can be observed in some people as they occur. During this period, it is also believed by some psychologists that humans also go through emotional changes every seven years. It is believed human beings go through various stages of growth, development, and change every seven years. If this is true, then it explains how at ages, 7, 14, 21, 28, 35, 42 and 49, we not only see physical change but experience major life changes at each different stage, which represent a new cycle of life. Just imagine the changes in relationships you have experienced every seven years from family and friends to new acquaintances and colleagues. Remember when you started kindergarten, entered middle school, transitioned into high school, or graduated college, entered the military, or simply became an adult. Those years flew by in seven-year increments. Think about when you met your spouse, started having children, started, lost, or quit jobs, bought or sold your home. All these events seemed to suddenly happen. We have all had relationships with others as children and watched as people have come in and out of our lives in phases, stages, and cycles. If you paid attention, you might have noticed that some, if not most, of those changes in relationships occurred about every seven years. Whether you notice it or not, we all are experiencing life in cycles of seven years at a time. As stated before, these cycles can be observed, tracked, and relied upon to occur in a specific manner and order. This is important because, as we discuss day and night, we must understand that the occurrence of day and night is a cycle.

Genesis 1:5 establishes the law of time with the first day being the foundation for time. This also establishes the foundation for the seven-day cycle called a week. The seven-day cycle establishes the foundation for the four-week cycle known as a month. This four-week cycle establishes the twelve-month cycle known as a year. The year repeats ten times to become a cycle known as a decade. The decade repeats ten times and becomes a cycle known as a century. The century repeats ten times and becomes a cycle known as a millennium. Each of these cycles originated with the twenty-four-hour cycle that begins with the evening and morning. You will also notice that not only does time repeat itself based on these cycles of time, but the human experience is repeated in cycles each generation. Ecclesiastes 1:4-7 describes in detail how cycles work. It states:

One generation passeth away, and another generation cometh; but the earth abideth forever. The sun also ariseth, and the sun goeth down, and hasteth to his place where he arose. The wind goeth toward the south, and turneth about unto the north, it whirleth about continually, and the wind returneth again according to his circuits. All the rivers run into the sea, yet the sea is not full; unto the place from whence the rivers come, thither they return again.

This group of scriptures explains that generations appear and pass away in cycles. The rising and setting of the sun occur in a cycle. The movement of the wind and clouds travels in a cyclical pattern. Even the rivers of water have a starting point and end or conclude at its place of origin, which is a cycle. The scriptures also tell us in Ecclesiastes 1:9: *The thing that hath been, it is that which shall be, and that which is done is that which shall be done: and there is no new thing under the sun.* In other words, what may seem or appear to be new to one generation is the repeating of events, patterns, or cycles for another generation. It is also said another way; what's old is what's new. These cycles or patterns are easily observed and recognized because they are based on the law of time.

This is important to recognize and to understand. Ecclesiastes 3:1 states: *To everything, there is a season and a time to every purpose under the heaven.* The word season is the Hebrew word (Zeman), which means a set time or an appointed time. In other words, everything in life is on God's timetable or God's schedule because everything has a set time or an appointed time when God wants or ordains for a thing to happen. God is the creator and architect of time, and time operates according to his schedule, not ours. Time is a function of creation, and time is also a tool and resource on earth. The word tool means anything used as a means of accomplishing a task or purpose. In other words, time is a means used by God to accomplish his work or his purpose on earth. You and I are given a certain amount of time to use to accomplish and fulfill our purpose on earth. As we begin to recognize this, we can begin to use our time more wisely, be more efficient and more effective. We can also begin to cooperate with God and agree with him so that we can become more fruitful in the earth. Consider this: when one period begins, another period ends. When a new cycle begins, an old cycle ends. When a leader dies or becomes too old to lead, a new leader emerges. When old ideas no longer produce wanted results, new ideas are sought out. When systems are archaic, rigid, or inflexible, they are soon replaced by newer, more efficient ones. Why? Because it's time for a change; an old cycle ends, and the time has come for a replacement.

Some cycles, however, repeat themselves. Some seasons repeat themselves. What is interesting and unique about cycles and seasons is that when they repeat, it is like someone getting a second chance to do what should have or could have been completed in the last cycle or last season. Sometimes, however, cycles and seasons can take years or decades before they repeat, which means you may have lost time, and time is the only commodity that we have that we cannot get more of. Therefore, time is not money, as some entrepreneurs, business owners, and investors would have us to believe. Time is Life, and Time is PRECIOUS. Time must be respected and used properly so that it is not wasted doing things that don't matter or that don't make a difference in life.

Time is so valuable that God says everything, and every purpose has a time set for it. From the moment we are born, to the moment we leave the earth, we have time measured out to us to complete or fulfill our purpose on earth. We, therefore, must use it wisely. Time is also a law that all living creatures are subject to and are all affected by. In the same manner, gravity is a law that all matter is subject to and affected by. When something is a law, it affects everyone, everywhere, all the time. These are natural and spiritual laws that all of creation is affected by, and these laws govern how we live our lives. These laws are established upon the foundation for what we call truth. Truth is original information from God, which is unchanging. Truth is the same in the past, present, and future. Truth becomes the basis for what we call wisdom. Wisdom is the ability to apply truth and law correctly. Wisdom is based on laws, and laws are based upon truth. Once you understand these principles, then life becomes easier to comprehend. This doesn't mean that every question or problem in the world is easily resolved by having this knowledge, but it does put life into perspective. It helps you to understand why some things happen; good or bad. You can begin to recognize patterns or cycles of behavior or events, and you can then begin to predict its certain outcome.

APPLYING THE CYCLE PRINCIPLE

When it comes to applying the principle of cycles, you will need to consider the following tips.

PRINCIPLE 1. Cycles are events or behaviors that we continuously repeat in life.

HOW TO APPLY PRINCIPLE 1. You must become proficient at recognizing patterns and sequences in your own life and in the events around you.

Cycles generally have patterns, phases, stages, sequences, signposts, or clues that are necessary to help you identify them. This means that a cycle will always repeat itself and must be recognized and identified based on its phases and stages to be useful to you. If you find yourself experiencing the same thing repeatedly, it is not déjà vu, you might be trapped in or living in a cycle that needs to be broken. An example of a cycle could be patterns of behavior that repeat themselves, which could be counter-productive, harmful, or even deadly in a persons' life. Someone may have a pattern of having financial challenges every six months to a year, no matter what kind of job they have or how much money they make. They may have a pattern of starting and ending relationships due to the same decision-making or patterns of behavior. They may have a pattern of starting new ventures that never get completed due to repeated behavior. They may experience the same negative consequences everywhere they live, even when they move to a new city.

PRINCIPLE 2. Cycles won't change until you decide to change them

HOW TO APPLY PRINCIPLE 2. Identify what phase or stage of the cycle you are in. Assess "How did I get here?" Evaluate "what have I done in the past when this happens, and what has been the outcome?" Ask, "what can I do differently so that I don't repeat the same behavior as before?"

These questions force you to look at your life and identify your ways of thinking, processing information, and decision-making that may be causing the repeating cycles in your life. There is also the issue of habits and past experiences that lead to the iteration or repetition of cycles in our lives. By following these steps, you will be able to assess where you are in the cycle, what happens in that phase of the cycle, and what usually happens next. This will also help you to recognize and identify what continues to occur in your life so that you can stop them from occurring again.

Principle 3. Habits create cycles that can work in your favor or work against you.

How to apply Principle 3. Make up your mind, take a stand, and choose what you will or will no longer do, settle for or tolerate in your own life, and create the kind of habits that change the cycles in your life. Be fully persuaded and resolved about your decision and commit to it. Make a quality decision about what you want in life instead of what you have been getting.

This means you will need to take responsibility and ownership for your life and stop self-sabotaging your life. This also means acknowledging that you are capable and well able to change the course of your life for the better. It may begin with you saying something like, "if I got myself into this mess, and I can get myself out."

Principle 4. Cycles require planning and preparation to enter and exit them.

How to apply Principle 4. Write down a plan of action that you will commit to and use to turn your situation around. Make sure your plans have deadlines for each benchmark you want to achieve. Start your plan with the end in mind and work your way backward. Make sure your plans also have a set of written goals, values, expectations, and behaviors to break the old cycle or patterns of behavior and to create new ones.

Also, monitor your progress and make adjustments when needed.

When you write a plan, you are creating a roadmap for yourself to follow, and you are deciding what you want to happen in your life and how you want it to look. A plan of action tells you what to do, when to do it, where you do it, how to do it, how long to do it, and, most importantly, why you are doing it. Your plan must also include the element of a deadline. This is important because not only do you want to come out of your negative situation, but you also want to give yourself a deadline to assess and measure your progress. Following or using a plan that is not designed to address your situation is counter-productive and a waste of your time. But as you begin to experience success, this will build up your confidence in your ability to solve your own problems and improve your life. Making plans, however, does not mean you do not consult God about your plan. In fact, the scriptures state in Proverbs 3:5-6, Trust in the Lord with all your heart and lean not to your own understanding. In all your ways acknowledge him, and he will direct your path. Proverbs 16:3 says, Share your plans with the Lord, and you will succeed. It also says in Proverbs 16:9, We make our own plans, but the Lord decides where we will go. If you are having difficulty creating your own plan, find a mentor or someone you trust and are willing to submit to, to make the necessary changes in your life.

Principle 5. Mentors can help you master the cycles of life.

How to apply Principle 5. Find a coach, mentor, or accountability partner to help you identify blind spots of your life that lead you into self-sabotaging life cycles and break the cycles/patterns of behavior

Having someone in your corner as a support system to help you win in life is crucial to navigating your life cycles. They help you identify the motives for your behavior and whether those behaviors and habits are helping or hindering your progress and success. Hopefully, they have a track record of success in their own lives and/or for helping others. If nothing else, they can at least tell you the truth and provide a dose of reality when you need to hear it. They can also help you ensure that your plan of action is specific to your situation to be useful and effective in navigating your way through the cycle(s) of life.

9

SUMMER AND WINTER (THE SEASON PRINCIPLE)

The next principle mentioned in Genesis 8:22 is that summer and winter shall not cease. The idea of summer represents fruitfulness, vibrancy, and productivity, while winter represents sterility, idleness, and barrenness. The idea most people have is usually the four seasons of the year. When you think of the winter, most times, people think of the blistering cold, blizzard-like conditions, arctic places like the South Pole or Antarctica, or other places where temperatures are frigid. In other parts of the world, it simply rains excessively and even becomes a monsoon. When you think of the summer, most people think of the hot sunny days, intense sun rays, hot air, and humidity. Some people think of dry arid environments like the Sahara Desert or similar places on earth. In America, when we think of summer, we think of the time of the year when people go swimming and travel on summer vacations. When we think of winter, we think of the times when people travel and spend the holidays with family and friends building snowmen, drinking hot cocoa, and bundling up under multiple layers of clothing to keep warm.

Summer and winter represent weather extremes created by God to accomplish specific things. First, winter represents a time of rest for nature. The temperatures are cold, which allows the land to rest and mammals to hibernate. The land can be depleted of nutrients immediately following a harvest of crops, and winter is a time of rest that allows for replenishing that which has been depleted. The summer is a time for growth and full development of vegetation and animal species. These are all examples of fixed or set periods or seasons. In the human family, humans don't develop physically as fast as animals and plant life. However, when physical growth and development in humans takes place, it's similar to what happens in the four seasons of the year. Between spring and summer is accelerated growth and development from the planting stage to the development of a root system in plants, crops, and other vegetation, which leads to the development of a stem. After this stage is the appearance of the blade of the crop, then the ear, and finally, the full corn in the ear, as stated in Mark 4:29. The summertime is the optimal time for growth and development of a planted seed, whereas the winter is the worst time for seed planting. This is establishing a process for growth and development of seeds sown or planted. It is also establishing a cycle that repeats each time a seed is sown, watered, and cultivated; it will eventually produce a crop or harvest in its season. This process and cycle do not occur during the winter months. This means there are optimal periods for sowing, planting and cultivating seeds, as well as optimal periods for resting, rejuvenation, and replenishing the land. You cannot sow or plant natural seeds during the winter season and expect a harvest. You can only do it during the springtime in most parts of the earth. The exceptions to this rule are the areas located near the equator where sowing and planting can occur all year long. In northern parts of the hemisphere, sowing and planting are seasonal. These are seasons and cycles which occur regularly and repeat themselves consistently with precision for those who cooperate with the system and process of seedtime and harvest.

Due to this point of reference, when most people hear the word season, they are not generally thinking of periods in a person's life when a drastic change occurs; but this is exactly what happens when you apply this principle to your life spiritually. The times in your life when unexpected things may seem to happen to come from out of nowhere is referred to as change. This interference or disruption is exactly what happens to indicate that your season is changing. The weather outside has not changed, but your personal season has. Sometimes a changing season may look like a sudden loss of employment after being on the job for many years. A new season could be the ending of a marriage, having a baby, children getting married, starting a business, writing a book, the death of a loved one, or any other host of things. The bottom line is your season has changed. This principle applies to both agriculture as well as spiritual reality. This also means when you are moved to act on an instruction from God, the season when you take action or sow your seed is your season for change and is the best time to sow. The word Season in Genesis 8:22 is the Hebrew word Zeman which means *a set time or an appointed time.*

In other words, a season is a set time or an appointed time. You can think of a season as being a moment in time that is scheduled, designated, or blocked out for a specified period. There are set times or appointed times when certain things occur. Sometimes seasons may last a few months or even a few years depending upon the situation. For example, certain phenomenon occurs during each season of the year that does not occur during others because the season is fixed, scheduled, designated, or blocked out for a specified period. When something is set, it is fixed. When something is appointed, it is predetermined or scheduled. In other words, seasons are fixed, predetermined, and scheduled by God to occur. Because seasons are fixed, predetermined, and scheduled by

God, this also means that seasons do not occur at the same time in all places.

The winter season is different in the northern hemisphere than in the southern hemisphere. The conditions for each season are also different depending upon where you are geographically. One location could be experiencing a season of drought while another one could be experiencing precipitation. Different places will experience different seasons at the same time of the year. This is true for people as well. Some people may be experiencing a season of productivity, increase, abundance, and promotion living their best lives, while others might be experiencing the exact opposite. This reality is sometimes expressed as being the best of times and the worst of times. Different groups of people can be having totally opposite experiences at the same time, but it is a different season for each group. This is because the seasons of our lives occur differently based on God's timetable for our lives, as well as the decisions we make.

In most cases, the seasons of our lives will be determined by the quality of our decisions. We know that life is choice driven, so when we make a decision, we invite change or a new season to enter our lives. When change occurs in our lives, it usually requires us to change, accept the change, learn and grow, from the change, or fight and resist the change. How we respond to the change may determine whether we experience a smooth transition of growth, stagnation, or heart-pounding fear and terror.

Sometimes a clear indication of a season-changing is when things stop working as they once did. When a light bulb burns out, it's time for a new light bulb. In other words, the season for the light bulb has ended, and it's time for a new one. When a company shuts down, you are left with a few options; leave with the company and go to the new location, stay and lose your job, go back to school and learn new skills, look for a new job, or maybe start a business or seek an entirely new career. In any case, you are experiencing a new season of life because your normal and daily routine has come to an end, and now you must start a new chapter in your life.

Ecclesiastes 3:1 states: *To everything, there is a season, and a time to every purpose under the heaven.* There are two take away points made in this scripture. The first principle is that everything has an appointed time to occur. The second point is that nothing is permanent. In other words, change is inevitable, and change is always happening. Change is the only permanent reality that we should expect in life. To say it another way, change is the only constant in the world. We can also see that change and seasons are also connected to purpose. What this means is that whenever change occurs, change is necessary. When life events happen, they usually change us or cause a change to occur within us. Sometimes that change is the ingredient necessary to help us change our perspective, our disposition, or our actions to become what we need to become or do what we need to do. This scripture is letting us know that everything has a season, and every purpose has a time. Every person has a purpose, and each purpose has a [set, fixed] time and an [appointed, scheduled] season for their expression and operation on earth. The [set] time or [appointed] season is the moment or period when the best fruit, the best expression, or the greatest manifestation of your purpose can be revealed. When that season is missed, you might go through other seasons or periods which may or may not repeat themselves as they would during a cycle. When your season is missed, it means you missed the window of opportunity where you have the greatest access to everything necessary to fulfill your created purpose. It also means you might not be at your best if or when the opportunity comes around again.

To illustrate the point, imagine that you are attempting to qualify for the Olympic team of your country. You have been practicing, training, conditioning, eating a restricted diet, and putting your mind and body through a process of becoming a world-class Olympic athlete. You have been living this life for many years because you want to be the best, and you have sacrificed everything to do it. Because the Olympics are held once every four years, a lot of things could happen to jeopardize your chances of qualifying for a spot on the team. Things such as injuries, better training tools, and techniques, a larger pool of competition, aging, younger athletes who may be stronger, faster, with greater endurance and stamina than you, or even other factors may eliminate your chances to qualify next time. Many Olympic athletes only compete in one Olympics Games because it requires a strict lifestyle of rigorous training, discipline, eating habits, and other regiments, making it difficult to have a normal life or a personal relationship. This pursuit for a spot on the Olympic team and a chance to win a medal all requires a singular focus on training, improving, competing, becoming the best, and winning. If a person has gone through this sort of self-denial for four, eight, twelve, or sixteen years, they may not want to continue along this way of life. They may want a family or some sense of normalcy and not pursue competition any further. These variables can and do affect the timing or season of when the athlete competes or for how long they compete, giving them a window of opportunity or a season as an Olympic athlete.

Sometimes starting a family, unexpected sickness, or death all could and sometimes does prevent people from getting into the competition to compete for the prize. Scripture tells us to redeem our time because the days are evil and that we are to not be unwise but [wise] understand[ing] what the will of the Lord is (Ephesian 5:16-17). Those seasons can also be enhanced by the decisions we make if we choose to cooperate with the leading and voice of God's spirit. An act of obedience can open the door to a season of abundance, blessing, and increase, which may last six months to three years. An act of obedience can also catapult you from anonymity into prominence. Things and events begin to happen in your life as if they were all time-sensitive and activated by the preceding act of obedience. It's as if a series of well-coordinated events "just happened" serendipitously with synchronicity. It's like driving down the street coming to a green light at every intersection, enabling you to get to your destination faster with less effort than you would if were running late and needing to drive faster. You wouldn't need to be in haste because you are early or on time, and everything is moving along smoothly. The opposite is also true. You might come to a red light and have to wait two to five minutes or two to five years, because of delay. One act of disobedience could lead to a year of delay, a decade of loss, stagnation, pain, misfortunes, missed opportunities, and suffering, leading one to think they are cursed, God is mad at them, or that the world is against them. These events tend to all work together when the timing or the season is right, or completely collapse and fall apart when the timing is wrong. A few illustrations of this principle regarding people being in their seasons are the elevation of public figures throughout history who seemed to appear out of nowhere and were suddenly thrust into the national and international scene. One example of timing is the case of Jesus Christ of Nazareth. Scripture proclaims in Galatians 4:4: But when the fullness of the time came, God sent forth his Son, made of a woman, made under the law.

This scripture tells us that Jesus came at the fullness of the time, or at the set time or appointed time. This Jewish carpenter turned rabbi appears on the national scene in Jerusalem at the age of thirty immediately following the incarceration of an eccentric preacher/prophet named John the Baptizer (Baptist). He picks up where John leaves off preaching a radically new message for their culture, referred to as The Kingdom of God, and he becomes more popular than John himself. He also becomes more influential than the established religious leaders of the day, which leads to jealousy and their diminished power and influence over the people. Not only is he disrupting the religious order of the day with a new paradigm for how people see themselves and see God, but he also demonstrates a superior level of wisdom and authority never seen before up to this time. He is demonstrating power and authority over time, space, and matter, and he tells his followers that they can do the same when they enter this Kingdom life and reality. This continues for three-and-a-half years, which leads up to him being falsely accused of insurrection and consequently being crucified by the Roman empire. This also sets the stage for him becoming the resurrected Savior he claimed to be when he was raised from the dead after three days, according to the scriptures. His resurrection not only increased his fame, but also made him and his name, the most well-known name in human history attracting more followers and becoming the founder of a new belief system called The Way, which is later called by pagans, Christianity. His life has been impacting the world for over two millenniums. It cannot be denied that Jesus was in his season. This was the case for Dr. Martin Luther King Jr., who completed and received his Ph.D. in Theological studies in 1955 and that same year joined the Civil Rights Movement of the south[58]. He later became the first president of the Southern Christian Leadership Convention and became one of the most prominent figures in the Civil Rights Movement (The King Center, 2019). Dr. King was not Jesus, but he was in his season. The meteoric political rise of Barack Hussein Obama from an Illinois state senator, to U.S. Senator, and then becoming a two-term U.S. president, and historic first African American President of the United States seems like a fantasy ("Barack Obama Biography," 2018). His story and obstacles are the makings of a true American story, yet his time in politics seemed to be undeniable; he was in his season. Many other figures hold a place in human history whose names and contributions to society are considered great and unforgettable, and what they all have in common is that they all were expressing their greatness because they were operating in their season.

APPLYING THE PRINCIPLE OF SEASONS

When it comes to applying the principle of seasons, it is necessary to understand the following set of tips.

PRINCIPLE 1. Seasons are all about understanding and recognizing spiritual timing.

HOW TO APPLY PRINCIPLE 1. Pray for awareness, understanding, and preparation about God's timing for your purpose.

Spiritual Timing means God's timetable and God's schedule for when things are set to happen or set to begin in a persons' life. Life has a rhythm, and Spiritual Timing also means that there is a rhythm to when and how things happen in a persons' life. Spiritual Timing is sometimes referred to as serendipity or luck, when favorable things happen to a person, seemingly by accident. An example of this occurs when you complete your education, training, or development in an area of study, and almost immediately, you meet someone at the coffee shop, at the gym, or at a gas station who requires your unique gift, talent, skill, ability, or experience. The encounter was not planned by you, yet you happened to be in the right place at the right time, meeting the right person. Spiritual Timing is also referred to as synchronicity, when a chain of events occurs in sequential order as if by coincidence. When this happens, your journey accelerates, and you experience promotion or elevation quickly along with financial increase, influence, and access to power or to those in power. Some may say you are on the fast track to success, but the truth is you have stepped into your season and

God's timing related to your purpose. However, you won't get to the next season of your life, if you don't pass the necessary tests to qualify to enter that season, and no doors of opportunity will open for you.

Principle 2. New seasons require the ability to adapt to change.

How to apply Principle 2. You must view change, interference, or disruption as signs of a new season and an opportunity to learn, grow, and develop your faith, character, or both.

Whenever change occurs, people have a tendency to fight the change, because most of us like things in our lives or around us to be stable or predictable. The challenge with the need for predictability is that change reveals that we are not always in control of every situation. This lack of control also exposes our vulnerability to change and reveals areas where improvements can be made in our lives, enabling us to develop our ability to adapt. This disruption can be unnerving to some people; it's like being in the midst of an earthquake when everything around us and under our feet is shaking, and our world appears to be falling apart. The good thing is that although earthquakes can be destructive, they are only temporary. They also force us to learn how not to panic in stressful situations, new ways of surviving and developing new skills of how to handle similar situations in the future, improving our chances of survival in the future. We learn from the experiences, adapt our behavior, grow in our understanding, and apply our wisdom in future situations.

Principle 3. Attacks against your character or demands on your gifts are signs of a new season

How to apply Principle 3. You must pass the tests of developing godly-character and stewardship of your gift before you move into your season.

What this means is that your gift can make room for you and take you places, but your character is necessary to keep you there. This also means that your character may be developed, but you have not matured in your gift to serve it to others at the level God intends. In either case, it means you are not yet ready to walk through the door leading to your purpose or destiny. This point is hard for many to accept, but it is true. Many gifted people in the world could occupy positions of influence or solve problems with their gifts, but they have terrible character and are like a walking contradiction. They are like an attractive, well-dressed man or woman with horrible hygiene. They are like a wealthy person who has no common sense. These people can do wonderful things with their gifts, but their poor character can sometimes diminish their respect and reputation in the eyes of the public. Your developed godly-character will be necessary to help you handle the pressure and the weight that will come along with the position or platform you occupy. You may have the ability to solve a problem with your gift, but you may never get that opportunity to prove it because of your poor character or poor stewardship of your gift.

Principle 4. Your season is activated by your decisions to move in the direction of your purpose.

. . .

How to Apply Principle 4. You must learn to make decisions in line with your purpose and not in line with your pleasure.

Your purpose necessitates that you make the right decisions or righteous decisions. When I say making the right decisions, I'm not just talking about you doing good things based on moral values or moral principles. I'm talking about you making the kind of decisions that make "the universe" respond to you with all of its resources because you are in alignment with God and his created purpose for your life. When you make the right decisions, you look like a genius to the rest of the world because your decision causes you to experience success at a supernatural pace. You see this happen when people make decisions to do something and take specific actions that cause them to go from being anonymous and obscure to becoming known worldwide. It's like going viral because you not only made a good decision, but you made a God decision. You are not just doing good things, but you are now doing God-ordained things. In other words, your decision turns on God's system for advancing or propelling you forward through something called favor. Favor is the principle of grace or unmerited blessing unleashed into your life, causing you to experience God's goodness, which you can never earn, ever deserve to have, or ever be able to purchase with money. Favor causes you to experience unfair advantages that others will never experience without God helping you. When favor is activated in your life, you appear to leap-frog over others into positions of authority who would normally need years to transition into. When you are in your season, the favor can be so strong that credentials, education, and experience sometimes are unnecessary to fit the role, but your gift and obedience to God is all that is needed to fulfill the role that requires you to be there. All of this and much more is the byproduct of a person being in the season of their purpose.

PRINCIPLE 5. Your season is signaled by increased demand for the use of your gift.

HOW TO APPLY PRINCIPLE 5. Your God-given abilities put on display reveal you are necessary for your position.

People don't necessarily love you, but they do love your gift. In other words, people love what your gift does for them. There is a scripture that states that your gift will make room for you and bring you before great men. What this means is that your gift is more important to God than your education, training, or experience. It is also more important to men, especially when your gift gets results. It also means that the process of preparing for your purpose only requires that you know how to use your gift correctly and that you have the heart and availability to please God and serve him where you are. This does not mean that God will put an irresponsible or unqualified person in a place of power or authority; however, it does mean that promotion comes from God, and he can open doors that no man can shut and close doors that no man can open. When your gift is needed, the circumstance will reveal to everyone that you are necessary to do a specific thing or fill a specific role that no one else can.

In an earlier chapter, I mentioned the story of Joseph, a Hebrew slave who had a gift that caused him to be elevated in one day from the prison to the palace and become second in command over all of Egypt next to the Pharaoh. There is a principle in mathematics which states, the shortest distance between two points is a straight line, and this is what happens when you are in your season. God can draw a straight line for you and put you exactly where you need to be without any hesitation, politics, compromising of morals and values, delay, or red tape. God can introduce you to the decision-maker who has an opportunity just for you that you are uniquely qualified for and are ready to step into. Another example is when you are moving in the direction of your purpose or your passion, and you start to make decisions or start meeting the exact people necessary to move you along the path in the pursuit of your destiny.

Spiritual Timing also involves synchronicity. When this occurs, it is similar to someone who uses a schedule to take a bus, a train, or a plane to get somewhere, and makes the necessary connections when they transfer to get to their desired destinations on time. The synchronicity of spiritual timing causes everything to line up in such a way that you happen to connect with just the right people at just the right time, taking you through just the right doors. The point here is not about chronology based on a clock or a calendar, but it is based on timing, on making the right decisions in line with your purpose and then connecting with people connected to your purpose. Your decisions in life with your purpose activates the next chain of events and opens the next set of doors for you to walk through, which leads you into the next season of your life.

10
THE JOURNEY (THE PROCESS PRINCIPLE)

The final principle to be discussed in this book is the journey or the PROCESS principle. When you read Genesis 8:22, what is being described is a set of principles, laws, and processes which God designed and created to be manifested on planet earth. A process is a continuous action, operation, or series of changes taking place in a definite manner. It is the action going forward, going on, or being carried on. In other words, a process is a series of steps, activities, and events which occur in a specific order to produce a specific result. All living matter goes through a series of steps or a process to reach full maturity or full manifestation. All mammals and living organisms go through a process to become what they become. You and I also went through a process to become who and what we are. A process can also be referred to as the journey of change and transformation. Anything that is created by God or man had to go through a process of becoming a completed entity or a finished product. From procreation and parenting, artistic expression, and ministry preparation, to entrepreneurship, mentoring, teaching, or leading a nation; everyone has or will go through a process or a journey to become themselves. The process of becoming oneself is sometimes called Self Actualization.

The process of Self Actualization is also necessary for anyone seeking to pursue and fulfill their mission in life or their purpose. The pursuit of purpose can never be fulfilled without first going through the process of preparation. I like to define and refer to the process of preparation as EDUCATION. To say it another way, EDUCATION is preparation for purpose. In my opinion, the definition for education must be preparation for purpose because if you are pursuing an education or training to do or become something which does not relate to your God-created purpose, then you or the student is being MISEDUCATED.

There are too many "miseducated" people running the world or occupying positions of influence and authority, who are not bringing honor or value to the positions they hold. They also are unable to experience the best and highest level of expression of who and what they are to become because they are in the wrong position. These people are not in "their lane," but in "someone else's lane." When someone is in the wrong lane, they usually are going the wrong way, or miss their turn, miss the exit ramp, block traffic, sometimes cause accidents for others or cause others or themselves to be killed. Not only is this true in terms of traveling along roads, streets, and highways, but this is also true in life. They have credentials from well-respected institutions, earned impressive advanced degrees of higher learning, and wear them like name brand clothing for all to see, which tells the world they are highly intelligent and very important. However, they are living a frustrated and defeated life because although they may command a hefty six-figure salary with bonuses, benefits, and other perks, they are not doing what God created them to do that affects the lives of those they are called to serve. They are doing what others expected of them or what others have told them they should be doing or what they might be good at doing. Some people are in certain occupations because they pursued a degree which promised or afforded prestige, social standing, fame, or a hefty salary. Again, this is not to suggest that education from the best or top universities is a bad or un-godly pursuit. It is not to insinuate that being ignorant or being a religious fanatic is the only way to please or serve God and serve people. It also is not a suggestion that to be in your lane or to operate in your purpose, you must be a pauper or take a vow of poverty. It is a warning, however, to anyone who pursues an endeavor for the wrong reasons. God does not have a problem with you having money. He doesn't want money to have you, your focus, your attention, your time, your energy, or your passion more than him or his purpose for your life. I have often heard it said that some people are just lucky in life and that opportunities happen for those that are lucky. I have also heard the definition for luck given by highly successful people as preparation meeting opportunity. Your decision could lead to a fantastic career and lifestyle, which may provide tremendous satisfaction to you and be a blessing to others. It could also lead to an unfulfilled life of regrets knowing that your time, talents, gifts, abilities, and potential were wasted on vain pursuits that have nothing to do with your God-created purpose. It's not that hard to figure out if you are doing what you want or what God wants you to do.

Ask yourself a few questions: How does my career, occupation, business, or endeavor to advance God's agenda here on earth? How am I using what I have been given by God to accomplish what I was sent to do in my generation? If you find yourself struggling to answer these questions, it simply means you are not doing what you want, or you have never considered bringing his will into the equation. Consider the reasons why you are in the career field you are presently in. Was/is the motivation behind your pursuit really the pursuit of a degree, intending to obtain a "good" job, with a high paying salary and "good" benefits? Was/is your decision based on knowing what you were/are born to do? Is the pursuit of your God-created purpose anywhere in that equation? Far too many well-meaning parents, coaches, mentors, ministers, and other caring adults have counseled young people to pursue a college education with no focus on pursuing their purpose. They advise young people to pursue obtaining success, which for many, is the pursuit of money, fame, status, and the American Dream. Many of these same well-meaning adults are repeating the same messaging, which they received from other well-meaning adults, and the cycle of misinformation is passed on to the next generation. This is not a knock against anyone who has obtained or is pursuing a college education. It is actually the opposite. It is an attempt to encourage everyone to pursue the best education, training, or preparation possible that will enable them to be fit and equipped to fulfill their purpose in life. This also means, however, each person will need to have a clear idea and understanding about their purpose before they head off to whatever education or training process or journey necessary.

Whenever you take the time to learn about high achievers or read the biographies of those who have accomplished great things in life, you will find in many cases, accomplishing the goal was not the most important factor. The greatest factor and the most fulfilling element in their story was their journey. The journey had more value to these high achievers because of the process they had to go through. Anyone who has competed in a triathlon, started a new business, raised healthy well-adjusted children, survived a critical illness, endured the loss of a child, became disabled, had a near-death experience or any other life-altering event has gone through a journey that affected them uniquely and permanently. Those who lived to tell their stories often speak of the dramatic transformation they went through and how their perspective on life has changed. For some, their experience made them optimistic about life and appreciated life and their loved ones more. For others, it made them pessimistic, cynical, jaded, and fearful. What all these scenarios have in common is that those events or processes have forever changed the way the individual thinks, believes, and lives their life. These processes of real-life events and experiences have created life lessons that shape how they see themselves and their worldview. These perspectives influence people to be bolder, more daring, and take more risks in life or to run in terror, shrink back, hide, or keep silent when challenged with similar obstacles. The experience of the journey often forces the individual to face their fears, learn about their triggers, their strengths, their weaknesses, as well as their own potential. After the journey is completed, the individual is introduced to the new version of themselves, which often shocks them. This new person may be less timid, more decisive, and now more action-oriented. Whatever the case may be, the old person is gone, and the new one has arrived to stay.

An additional point to consider is how others around this individual are affected by the process of change they went through. The nature and length of the relationship may determine how family, friends, and acquaintances respond. If the person was once passive, timid, and shy, and now is infused with a sudden boost of boldness, this could be disruptive and traumatic for those closest to the individual. The transformed person may no longer respond in the traditional way they responded before, and if they were accommodating or acquiesced when approached or challenged and now respond with formidable resolve, it would change the dynamics of the relationship.

COLD AND HEAT (THE PROCESS PRINCIPLE CONTINUED)

Genesis 8:22 mentions that cold and heat shall not cease. This principle is describing a process. This principle lets us know that there are changes that occur atmospherically, ecologically, and agriculturally, that will always occur. Allow me here to restate what a process is. A process is a continuous action, operation, or series of changes taking place in a definite manner. It is the action going forward, going on, or being carried on. In other words, processes are events, actions, and activities that bring about continuous change in a definite manner. Process is the word we use to describe when a person, place, or thing undergoes any type of change, development, training, improvement, upgrade, or transformation. Whenever something is being changed from one thing into another, we say it is going through a process or is in transition. Most processes can be observed, tracked, and evaluated or assessed to determine how much of a change has occurred. Anything and everything that goes through a process does so over time because PROCESSES TAKE TIME. Whenever someone is going through a process, they go through or experience a series of steps as they develop a new regular routine of actions. They begin to experience a new normal. Sometimes those actions are daily, weekly, or monthly. The reason why processes take time is that our daily routines or habits take anywhere from 18 to 66 days to develop (Rubin, 2009). Your mind and muscle memory are conditioned, trained, and developed to do things the same way all the time. We call these repetitive activities "habits," and those habits took time to develop. Breaking habits is a process and can also take a long time, so if you are undisciplined, don't expect to be able to suddenly break that habit. Developing new habits is also a process and takes time to implement. Learning new information is a process. Learning new skills is a process. Learning new ways of doing things is a process. Starting a business, developing discipline, training, and developing leaders is a process. As I have been writing this book, I have also undergone a process of writing, reading, rewriting, rereading, editing, reading, inserting, rewording, deleting, writing some more, reading some more, modifying, summarizing, simplifying, more writing and modifying. Sometimes a process can be disruptive, uncomfortable, painful, and affect everything or everyone around or near it.

Everything and everyone on earth undergoes a process to become what it or they become. Sometimes other words are used to describe a process; words like transformation or metamorphosis. One of the best illustrations of a process, transformation, or metamorphosis that most people are familiar with is that of the caterpillar becoming a butterfly. It is one of the most powerful examples of a process because the change or transformation is physical, visual, and dramatic. A creature, which was once small, insignificant, and limited to crawling at an exceedingly slow rate of speed, builds a cocoon, undergoes a process and transformation, and comes out as a beautifully colored butterfly. This process and transformation is not based on appearance alone but also based on function and ability. This new being can now fly, which it could never do before the change and transformation, which are all part of the process. This insect literally becomes a new creature or new creation, and life for this creature will never be the same. What is important to know here is that processes occur in all facets of life. Processes occur daily in every area of nature, in human beings, in manufacturing, in learning and education, in innovation, technological development, etc. In fact, it would difficult to locate any area of existence known to man where processes or changes are not occurring. Whether something is being created, manufactured, modified, altered, improved, deconstructed, or destroyed, each one of these stages is part of a process.

When we use words like cold or heat, the words themselves describe polar-opposite changing conditions that are part of a process in the atmosphere related to weather phenomena. These changes are necessary for the ecosystem on planet earth and in seedtime and harvest. Conditions of cold and heat affect the seed and environment, or the atmosphere where the seed is sown, causing an explosion of growth for plant life, vegetation, and other forms of life. Sometimes extreme weather conditions affect the outcome of the harvest, causing a delay in growth or some other adverse effect on the seed or the harvest. Regardless of weather conditions, processes will continue to occur, and whatever the outcome is, a process occurred leading up to that end effect. For example, a rainy season can accelerate the growth of a harvest or destroy it due to excessive rain. An extreme cold season could potentially halt growth, development, and the intended increase. Differences in the atmosphere affect the environment and influences what happens to life on earth. These weather conditions make it possible for sowing and planting to occur, which leads to crop production and harvest at the end of that season. On the opposite end of the spectrum, cooler temperatures enable the soil and the land to rest, recuperate, and replenish the depleted nutrients for the next seasonal change. This principle of planting and sowing seeds for crop production is part of the process which occurs within cycles and is time-sensitive.

Some similarities occur in our lives personally, professionally, and otherwise. For example, when you are in the right environment, some of your innate abilities and dormant potential come to life, revealing possibilities in areas that you may never had considered exploring. When this happens, people may say you're "hot," or you are "on fire" or "in the zone," or "in your lane" or "doing your thing." These abilities are being put on display because you're are in the right environment, or conditions are right for you to soar and flourish. Those seeds of greatness have the opportunity to grow and blossom. The opposite might also be true when no matter what you do, things aren't working. It's like you hit a dead end, or you've come to the end of the road because everything is cold. Those seeds of potential might not be getting what is needed to reveal their potential in you. The timing could be off, or you might be having a bad "string of luck." Whatever you might want to call it, it is evident you are not hot, but rather you are very cold.

APPLYING THE PROCESS PRINCIPLE

To apply the process principle, it is necessary to understand the following tips.

PRINCIPLE 1. All processes take time to develop.

HOW TO APPLY PRINCIPLE 1. Exercise patience and do not rush during the journey.

This is important to understand because unless you have never designed processes in the past, you may not be clear on what it will take to produce what you want or need. Time is always necessary with any kind of process to figure out any nuances in the process or what will enable a process to work properly.

PRINCIPLE 2. Processes must have steps developed and applied properly to achieve the desired results.

HOW TO APPLY PRINCIPLE 2. Document your actions and record the outcome of your progress.

This helps you to see the process in action and know if or where adjustments need to be made. When you understand this, it helps you to not be anxious, hasty, or in a rush to get things done, or get to the final product in a hurry. Consider something like wine, which takes time to age properly before it can be consumed. Think about the process of a planted seed, becoming a mature crop. Think about the process of a baby becoming a full-grown adult. Think about the process necessary for making cheese, building a house, raising children, starting and building a thriving, profitable business, or anything else that took months or years to fully develop.

PRINCIPLE 3. Concepts and processes must be proven to work consistently.

HOW TO APPLY PRINCIPLE 3. Do the work necessary to validate your proof of concept & processes.

Everything undergoes a process before it can be put on display. What this means is that every process must be proven to determine if it works properly and correctly to produce the intended results. If the process works correctly, it will be proven by the quality and integrity of the product. Even if you don't know every step at the beginning, you need to map out a blueprint for what you will do, where you want to go, and how you will get there. Developing your process, in itself, will be a process because there will probably be things that pop up that you didn't anticipate that might hinder you or slow you down. You will be developing, correcting, modifying, and adjusting all the way until you and your team come up with something that works. Don't worry about making mistakes, miscalculations, or errors in judgment. Just know that it's all part of the process. As you go along this journey, you will learn about what works and what doesn't. You will learn about yourself and how you react or respond to challenges, conflicts, obstacles, barriers, opposition, modifications, budgets, deficits, deadlines, and a whole host of other things designed to test your resolve and commitment to going through the process. In the end, there is a possibility that you might not recognize yourself simply because as you went through the process of creating, developing, and building, you might discover that you also went through a process of learning, growing, and developing into a new and better version of yourself. This is the goal of processes; becoming better and being a whole new creature.

Principle 4. Processes must be duplicatable for others to achieve the same results.

How to Apply Principle 4. Imitate the steps of others who have achieved what you desire to achieve and do not deviate.

In other words, success leaves crumbs. Whatever you intend to do, you must have a clear idea of what the end will be or what it will look like. Whenever you follow the steps of others who achieve their goals consistently, you have more confidence that your actions will produce the desired expectations. When you can achieve consistent results, others can begin to do the same. Some processes are subjective to different kinds of experiences, but if someone intends to duplicate success, the process must be duplicatable.

Principle 5. Processes change the person along the journey.

. . .

HOW TO APPLY PRINCIPLE 5. Be committed and willing to go through the process.

Because processes take time, require patience, have a series of steps to be completed, must be proven to work consistently, and be duplicatable, the person going through process becomes transformed in their way of thinking, their habits, their behavior, their worldview, and their expectations. As a result of all of this, they become a new person because of the journey or the process.

S.C.S.P. SUMMARY

We have come to the conclusion of our journey called Systems, Cycles, Seasons, and Processes: Understanding and Applying the Law of Seedtime and Harvest. This author has intended to share a few of the principles and laws that govern both the spiritual realm and the earth realm that may have had an impact on your life and the lives of those you love and care for. This author has intended to illustrate what the principles are and how to apply them to your life, relationships, and all that you do. If you have come this far, congratulations. Now you know some of the factors that may have been hindering you, holding you back, or assisting you and advancing you towards success. It is my prayer that your life has been impacted, empowered, elevated, and advanced into God's plan and purpose for your life as you have read, meditated, studied, and applied the contents of this book. May you now begin to experience God's Best for your life and your journey in revealing him and his kingdom to the world through your sphere of influence.

SWITCHING SYSTEMS, SWITCHING ALLEGIANCES

As you have read through this book, you learned many principles based on the word of God designed by God and for the benefit of Gods' people. There is the possibility, however, that you might not be properly positioned as a child of God, as a disciple of Christ, or as a Kingdom Citizen. If this is the case, I have GOOD NEWS! The scriptures teach according to Romans 10:9-10, that if thou shalt confess with thy mouth the Lord Jesus, and shalt believe in thine heart that God hath raised him from the dead, thou shalt be saved. For with the heart man believeth unto righteousness, and with the mouth confession is made unto salvation. It also teaches according to Colossians 1:13-14 that God, hath delivered us from the power of darkness, and hath translated us into the kingdom of his dear Son: In whom we have redemption through his blood, even the forgiveness of sins. What this means is that you can make a change TODAY by surrendering your life to God and receiving his son Jesus, Yeshua, as your Lord, and as Savior of your Life. Simply repeat this prayer out loud and mean it from your heart.

Dear God in Heaven, I come to you with a need to acknowledge that I am a sinner, in need of a Savior. Your word says, Him that comes to me, I will in no ways cast out, so I know you won't cast me out, but you will take me in, and I thank you for it. You said in your word that if I confess with my mouth, the Lord Jesus, and shall believe in my heart, that God raised him from the dead, for my justification, I would be saved. I am confessing with my mouth, and I believe in my heart that Jesus is the Son of God, who died on the cross for my sins, and was raised from the dead for my justification. I repent of my sin, and I receive Him right now, as my Lord, and as my Savior! You also said in your word that if I asked for the Holy Spirit, you would give him to me. Father, I ask you to fill me right now with your Holy Spirit. Holy Spirit, come inside me. Lead me, teach me, guide me, direct my life, reveal to me my purpose, my identity, my gifts, and show me how to live for you and fulfill your purpose for my life. Thank you, Father, for saving me, and filling me, with your Holy Spirit, in Jesus (Yeshua) Name I pray, AMEN!

If you prayed that prayer and meant it from your heart, you have just taken the first major step to experience the reality of God in your life. Congratulations, and welcome to the Kingdom of God. I would encourage you to ask God to lead you to a Bible-believing, Bible-teaching, Disciple-making, Spirit-filled church where you can begin the journey of walking out your purpose as a disciple of Christ. For your benefit, I have extracted the principles from each chapter and section of the book so that you are clear on what they are, can refer back to them, and be sure you are applying them correctly. Enjoy!

APPLYING THE SYSTEM PRINCIPLE

Principle 1. Find a system that produces the kind of results you want to be duplicated in your own life, or create, design, and implement your own system.

Principle 2. Have a definite starting point and a definite ending point to produce the product, service, or results you want.

Principle 3. Your system must have the ability to produce results efficiently, making things easier, better, and faster; this is what systems do.

Principle 4. Your system must have the ability to create leverage.

Principle 5. Your system must give you the ability to control the process and outcomes at will.

Principle 6. Your system must have the capacity to be automated. In other words, it must be able to function with little to no effort from anyone.

Principle 7. Your system must have the ability to manage resources, allowing you the ability to free up time in other areas giving you your time back.

APPLYING OBEDIENCE PRINCIPLE

Principle 1. You must know how to interpret scripture, since the scriptures give you the keys, laws, and secrets to the principles of obedience.

Principle 2. Pray and ask God to reveal how these scriptures apply to you and show you how to apply them to your own life.

Principle 3. You must expect God to speak to you and know how he speaks.

Principle 4. God knows the future, and you and I don't. He is worthy and deserving to be heard.

Principle 5. You must choose to obey God.

Principle 6. You must discern God's timing if you are to act immediately or wait for other instructions.

Principle 7. Complete every instruction God gives so that you are not operating in partial obedience, or delayed obedience.

APPLYING TIME PRINCIPLE

Principle 1. Ask God what your purpose is and how you should use your time.

Principle 2. Write out a plan of action to pursue your purpose (S.M.A.R.T Goal).

Principle 3. Be highly selective of who you allow into your life and have access to your time.

Principle 4. Surround yourself with others who are purpose-driven and who have a sense of focus and destiny in their lives.

Principle 5. Be discriminating in whom you receive and accept advice, counsel, and input from.

APPLYING FAITH PRINCIPLE

Principle 1. Acting in faith begins where the will of God is known.

Principle 2. Activate God's promises in your life by speaking his promises over your life daily.

Principle 3. Take action on what you believe based on the written and spoken word of God.

APPLYING THOUGHT PRINCIPLE

Principle 1. You must first identify what you are thinking about or identify your own thoughts.

Principle 2. Consider if what you are thinking is helpful or harmful to you or your situation.

Principle 3. Align your thinking with scriptural standards.

Principle 4. Begin immersing yourself in the scriptures.

APPLYING WORDS AS SEEDS

Principle 1. Words have the power of life or death.

Principle 2. Words express your thinking and emotional state.

Principle 3. You will only have what you say, not what others say.

Principle 4. God confirms his word with signs following, so speak His word.

APPLYING GIVING

Principle 1. Giving is a Law, and everyone can be a Giver.

Principle 2. Decide that you will be a generous giver.

Principle 3. Be intentional about what you give and how you give.

Principle 4. Never allow your giving to be conditional or with strings attached.

Principle 5. Giving is a heart issue.

Principle 6. Giving demonstrates the heart of God.

APPLYING SOWING

Principle 1. Sowing is God-directed giving.

Principle 2. Sowing is an act of obedience.

Principle 3. Sowing is not an emotional event.

Principle 4. Obey completely.

APPLYING CYCLE PRINCIPLE

Principle 1. Cycles are events or behaviors that we continuously repeat in life.

Principle 2. Cycles won't change until you decide to change them

Principle 3. Habits create cycles that can work in your favor or work against you.

Principle 4. Cycles require planning and preparation to enter and exit them.

Principle 5. Mentors can help you master the cycles of life.

APPLYING THE SEASON PRINCIPLE

Principle 1. Seasons are all about understanding and recognizing spiritual timing.

Principle 2. New seasons require the ability to adapt to change.

Principle 3. Attacks against your character or demands on your gifts are signs of a new season.

Principle 4. Your season is activated by your decisions to move in the direction of your purpose.

Principle 5. Your season is signaled by increased demand for the use of your gift.

APPLYING THE PROCESS PRINCIPLE

Principle 1. All processes take time to develop.

Principle 2. Processes must have steps developed and applied properly to achieve the desired results.

Principle 3. Concepts and processes must be proven to work consistently.

Principle 4. Processes must be duplicatable for others to achieve the same results.

Principle 5. Processes change the person along the journey.

ABOUT THE AUTHOR

Marcus "Emjay" Smith is a life-long learning who seeks truth, applies truth, and teaches truth that expands minds, challenges traditions, and transforms lives. As a bible teacher, financial literacy instructor, public speaker, and mentor to millennials & centennials, Emjay delivers his unique style of spiritual education that teaches, empowers, and prepares audiences to pursue and fulfill their purpose in life.

He has published his first book entitled *Systems, Cycles, Seasons, & Processes: Understanding and Applying the Law of Seed, Time, and Harvest.* Emjay currently lives in St. Louis with Tammie, his wife of twenty-five years and serves as Adjunct Instructor at St. Louis Community College and financial services professional.

ACKNOWLEDGMENTS

I would like to thank and acknowledge those dear friends, family, and loved ones who helped, encouraged, or in some way contributed to this work and labor of love.

To my loving and beautiful wife Tammie Smith, thank so much for your love, support, encouragement, and assistance in helping me to stay on track and making sure no one was a distraction and checking my prayer journal so that I would write what God said to write and not just what I wanted to. Thank you to C.P. Howard for allowing me space in your home to actually write the book for months and for providing candid, and sometimes brutal honesty about what I needed to hear about the book, and not just what I wanted to hear. To Keith Turner; a servant and mentor to the next generation, an author, businessman, and leader in the St. Louis region. Thank you for your support, contribution, example, and encouragement joining you as an author. To Rachel Jackson; thank you for your sharp and keen eye and attention to detail and feedback on this project. To Karen Helm: thank you, big sis, for your invaluable encouragement and making me want to get the book completed. To Rhonda McAlister; you made me feel like a bestselling author when you read the first draft. Thank you so much. To Alphonso Ivy Jr, and Latour Winston; two spiritual and intellectual giants in my book. Thank you for your wise insight and suggestions for this and the upcoming works. I cannot thank either of you enough for your contribution. To Bridget Riddle; thank you for the questions, conversations, and insight that made SCSP what it is today. To Melvin Davis; thank you for your friendship today and during the days at BGCSTL, and for your words of wisdom, support, and encouragement in this work. To Tiweon "Tee-Smooth" Henderson; Myyy Dude! Nuff said! To Latecia Clay; you are the definition of an independent woman who gets things done, and with all that, you still had time to read, enjoy and provide valuable feedback on my book, love you, sis. To my church family of G2GCC, thank you for your love every week and for being the reason why I wanted to write this book. To my pastor, Dr. Alfred D. Harvey Jr.; thank you, pastor, for your example as a man of God who is not perfect, but consistent in your example, and thank you for teaching me and my family how to rightly divide the word, stand on the word and be doers of the word. To all my family, (too many of y'all to name) of Smith, Silas, Crenshaw, Herndon, Bell, Anderson, Boyd, and Simmons, thank you all for your unfailing and unceasing love and support. Lastly, to my friend and mentor Samuel Solomon; you sir have been one of the most significant tools of learning, growth, change, and transformation in my life. I thank God for you, your friendship, your work, your family, your example and your influence that encouraged and challenged me to become an author, value creator, and leader who is comfortable with thinking, speaking, doing, and living differently than others around me. I love you and your family very much.

REFERENCES

Barack Obama Biography (2018). Retrieved from https://www.biography.com/us-president/barack-obama

Barufaldi, D. (2019). A Review Of Past Recessions. Retrieved from https://www.investopedia.com/articles/economics/08/past-recessions.asp

Cahn , J. (2014). *The Mystery of Shemitah: The 3,000-Year-Old Mystery That Holds the Secret of America's Future, the World's Future, and Your Future.* : Charisma Media.

Chowdhury, K. (2014). Outsiders in Ferguson. Retrieved from https://www.counterpunch.org/2014/08/21/outsiders-in-ferguson/

Crilly, Allen, Khan, Alexander, R. N. M. H. (2014). Ferguson riots: latest. Retrieved from https://www.telegraph.co.uk/news/worldnews/northamerica/usa/11252132/Ferguson-riots-live.html

Friedersdorf, C. (2015). A Tough Weekend for the Black Lives Matter Movement. Retrieved from https://www.theatlantic.com/politics/archive/2015/08/a-tough-weekend-for-the-black-lives-matter-movement/400862/

Gladwell, M. (2008). *Outliers: The Story of Success*. New York, New York: Little, Brown and Company.

Gray, R. (2019). A Former Alt-Right Member's Message: Get Out While You Still Can. Retrieved from https://www.buzzfeednews.com/article/rosiegray/katie-mchugh

Grunge. (n.d.). Musicians who predicted their own deaths. Retrieved from https://www.grunge.com/125455/musicians-who-predicted-their-own-deaths/

Gun sales spike around Ferguson after 3 days of riots (2015). Retrieved from https://www.rt.com/usa/180084-gun-sales-ferguson-protests/

History.com. (2018). 9/11 Attacks. Retrieved from https://www.history.com/topics/21st-century/9-11-attacks

Investopedia. (2019). Identifying Market Trends. Retrieved from https://www.investopedia.com/articles/technical/03/060303.asp

King Jr. , Dr. M. L. (August 28, 1963). "*I Have a Dream,*" *Address Delivered at the March on Washington for Jobs and Freedom.* Washington, D.C., Washington, D.C.: The Martin Luther King, Jr. Research and Education Institute.

Mercer, Macaulay, C. T. (2019). Which companies are making driverless cars?. Retrieved from https://www.techworld.com/picture-gallery/data/-companies-working-on-driverless-cars-3641537/

Newton's Third Law (n.d.). Retrieved from https://www.physicsclassroom.com/class/newtlaws/Lesson-4/Newton-s-Third-Law

Pruitt, S. (2018). Here Are 6 Things Albert Einstein Never Said. Retrieved from https://www.history.com/news/here-are-6-things-albert-einstein-never-said

Rubin, G. (2009). Stop Expecting to Change Your Habit in 21 Days. Retrieved from https://www.psychologytoday.com/us/blog/the-happiness-project/200910/stop-expecting-change-your-habit-in-21-days

Sales, B. (2014). Understanding Shmita, Israel's agricultural Shabbat. Retrieved from https://www.jta.org/2014/09/09/israel/understanding-shmita-israels-agricultural-shabbat-1

Suggs, E. (2014). The Michael Brown killing: What you need to know. Retrieved from https://www.ajc.com/news/ferguson-brown-faq/

The King Center. (2019). About Dr. King. Retrieved from https://thekingcenter.org/about-dr-king/

OTHER EDUMATCH TITLES

EduMatch Snapshot in Education (2016)
In this collaborative project, twenty educators located throughout the United States share educational strategies that have worked well for them, both with students and in their professional practice.

The #EduMatch Teacher's Recipe Guide
Editors: Tammy Neil & Sarah Thomas
Dive in as fourteen international educators share their recipes for success, both literally and metaphorically!

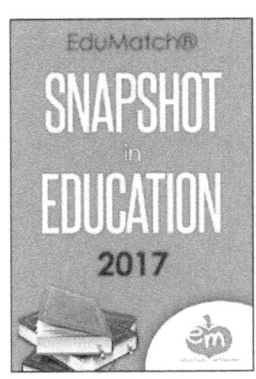

EduMatch Snapshot in Education (2017)
We're back! EduMatch proudly presents Snapshot in Education (2017). In this two-volume collection, 32 educators and one student share their tips for the classroom and professional practice.

Journey to The "Y" in You by Dene Gainey
This book started as a series of separate writing pieces that were eventually woven together to form a fabric called The Y in You. The question is, "What's the 'why' in you?"

The Teacher's Journey by Brian Costello
Follow the Teacher's Journey with Brian as he weaves together the stories of seven incredible educators. Each step encourages educators at any level to reflect, grow, and connect.

The Fire Within
Compiled and edited by Mandy Froehlich
Adversity itself is not what defines us. It is how we react to that adversity and the choices we make that creates who we are and how we will persevere.

EduMagic by Sam Fecich
This book challenges the thought that "teaching" begins only after certification and college graduation. Instead, it describes how students in teacher preparation programs have value to offer their future colleagues, even as they are learning to be teachers!

Makers in Schools
Editors: Susan Brown & Barbara Liedahl
The maker mindset sets the stage for the Fourth Industrial Revolution, empowering educators to guide their students.

Divergent EDU by Mandy Froehlich
The concept of being innovative can be made to sound so simple. But what if the development of the innovative thinking isn't the only roadblock?

EduMatch Snapshot in Education (2018)
EduMatch® *is back for our third annual Snapshot in Education. Dive in as 21 educators share a snapshot of what they learned, what they did, and how they grew in 2018.*

Daddy's Favorites by Elissa Joy
Illustrated by Dionne Victoria
Five-year-old Jill wants to be the center of everyone's world. But, her most favorite person in the world, without fail, is her Daddy. But Daddy has to be Daddy, and most times that means he has to be there when everyone needs him, especially when her brother Danny needs him.

Level Up Leadership by Brian Kulak

Gaming has captivated its players for generations and cemented itself as a fundamental part of our culture. In order to reach the end of the game, they all need to level up.

DigCit Kids edited by Marialice Curran & Curran Dee

This book is a compilation of stories, starting with our own mother and son story, and shares examples from both parents and educators on how they embed digital citizenship at home and in the classroom.

Stories of EduInfluence by Brent Coley

In *Stories of EduInfluence*, veteran educator Brent Coley shares stories from more than two decades in the classroom and front office.

The Edupreneur by Dr. Will

The Edupreneur is a 2019 documentary film that takes you on a journey into the successes and challenges of some of the most recognized names in K-12 education consulting.

In Other Words by Rachelle Dene Poth
In Other Words is a book full of inspirational and thought-provoking quotes that have pushed the author's thinking and inspired her.

To Whom it May Concern
Editors: Sarah-Jane Thomas, PhD & Nicol R. Howard, PhD
In To Whom it May Concern..., you will read a collaboration between two Master's in Education classes at two universities on opposite coasts of the United States.

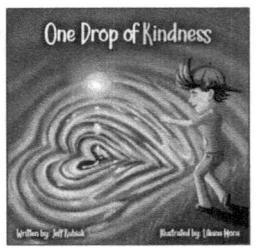

One Drop of Kindness by Jeff Kubiak
This children's book, along with each of you, will change our world as we know it. It only takes One Drop of Kindness to fill a heart with love.

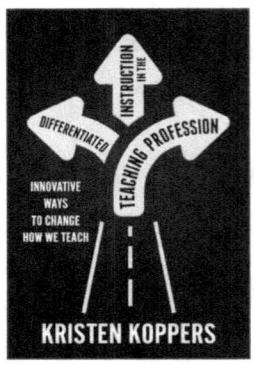

Differentiated Instruction in the Teaching Profession by Kristen Koppers
Differentiated Instruction in the Teaching Profession is an innovative way to use critical thinking skills to create strategies to help all students succeed. This book is for educators of all levels who want to take the next step into differentiating their instruction.

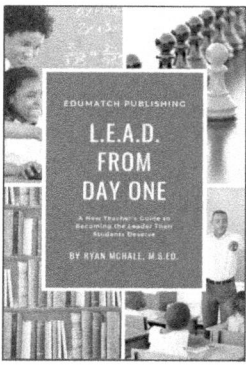

L.E.A.D. from Day One by Ryan McHale

L.E.A.D. from Day One is a go-to resource to help educators outline a future plan toward becoming a teacher leader. The purpose of this book is to help you see just how easily you can transform your entire mindset to become the leader your students need you to be.

Unlock Creativity by Jacie Maslyk

Every classroom is filled with creative potential. Unlock Creativity will help you discover opportunities that will make every student see themselves as a creative thinker.

Make Waves! by Hal Roberts
In *Make Waves!* Hal discusses 15 attributes of a great leader. He shares his varied experience as a teacher, leader, a player in the N.F.L., and a plethora of research to take you on a journey to emerge as leader of significance.

21 Lessons of Tech Integration Coaching by Martine Brown
In *21 Lessons of Tech Integration Coaching*, Martine Brown provides a practical guide about how to use your skills to support and transform schools.

Everyone Can Learn Math by Alice Aspinall
How do you approach a math problem that challenges you? Do you keep trying until you reach a solution? Or are you like Amy, who gets frustrated easily and gives up?

EduMagic Shine On by Sam Fecich, Katy Gibson, Hannah Sansom, and Hannah Turk
EduMagic: A Guide for New Teachers picks up where EduMagic: A Guide for Preservice Teachers leaves off. Dr. Sam Fecich is back at the coffee shop and is now joined by three former students-turned-friends. She is excited to introduce you to these three young teachers: Katy Gibson, Hannah Sansom, and Hannah Turk.

Unconventional by Rachelle Dene Poth

Unconventional will empower educators to take risks, explore new ideas and emerging technologies, and bring amazing changes to classrooms. Dive in to transform student learning and thrive in edu!

All In by Kristen Nan & Jacie Maslyk

Unlike Nevada's slogan of "what happens in Vegas, stays in Vegas," this book reminds us that what happens in the classroom, should never stay within the classroom!

EduMatch Snapshot in Education 2019
EduMatch® is back for our fourth annual Snapshot in Education. Dive in as an international crew of educators share a snapshot of what they learned, what they did, and how they grew in 2019. Topics include Social Emotional Learning, identity, instructional tips, and much more!

Play? Yay! by BreAnn Fennell
Play? Yay! is a book my mom wrote for kids. I'm a toddler, and I like to read. I sit and look at pictures or point to my favorite pages. Do you like books like that? Then this book is for you too! The best part about this book is that you can read it with people like moms, dads, or grandparents. Get *Play? Yay!* today for fun, rhymes, and the gift of imagination.

The EdCorps Classroom by Chris Aviles

Something happens when you launch an EdCorps in your classroom. An EdCorps, or Education Corporation, is what you get when you teach your curriculum through entrepreneurship. In this how-to guide, Chris Aviles tells you how he accidentally stumbled into the world of student-run businesses, and how you can use them to provide authentic learning to your students.

Strive by Robert Dunlop

This book will get you thinking about how happy you are in your career and give you practical strategies to make changes that will truly impact your happiness. Packed with research and inspiring stories, you will end each chapter inspired and excited to try new job-embedded ways to find more joy at work.

Thinking About Teaching by Casey Jakubowski

Teaching is by far one of the most intellectually rewarding, emotionally challenging, and physically exhausting careers in the world. This book explores the thoughts that author Casey T. Jakubowski, PhD has on a wide range of education related topics. Seeking to give voice to rural education, in this unstable time, and reflecting on a wide of research and experiences, this work offers all educators, from the beginning, all the way to the end, a reflective voice to channel their own experiences against and with on their journey.

I'm Sorry Story by Melody McAllister

Do you know what it's like to sit by yourself at lunch? Do you know how it feels when it seems everyone around you has close friends except you? That's exactly how Ryan feels. He wants good friends and he wants to be accepted by his classmates, but he isn't sure how to make that happen. Join him as he learns to put others first and make things right when he has been wrong!

Define Your Why by Barbara Bray

Barbara Bray wrote Define Your WHY from the process she went through to figure out her WHY and through coaching others who did not feel valued, appreciated, or why they needed to live on purpose. Barbara tells her story with stories from 26 inspirational thought leaders along with quotes, resources, questions, and activities to help you on your journey to define your WHY so you own your story.

To the Edge by Kyle Anderson

Follow Kyle through his trials and tribulations in risk-taking. Throughout To The Edge, Kyle shares his story of how risks have shaped him into the person and educator that he is today. From risks that resulted in immediate success to ones that elicited failure and regret, you surely will be inspired by Kyle's story. Take yourself to the edge and become more of a risk-taker in your life and career! #ToTheEdgeEDU

www.ingramcontent.com/pod-product-compliance
Lightning Source LLC
Chambersburg PA
CBHW071240070526
44583CB00017B/2271